MW00717014

PRAISE FOR *HOUSE CALLS w*

House Calls with Jesus is a remarkable text. I read it from cover to cover in one sitting with tears in my eyes and a prayer in my heart. This book is gritty and graceful. Death isn't easy and this text doesn't shy away from pain and desolation. But, it is ultimately joyful in tone, joyful because on every page we discover that God's love, and the love we have for each other, is stronger than death, and that nothing, not even death and debilitation, can separate us from the love of God. I highly recommend this book for pastors, hospice chaplains, nurses and physicians, and family members of persons facing life-threatening and incurable illness. There is hope and it comes from walking through the valley of the shadow of death and knowing that God is with us.

Dr. Bruce G. Epperly
author, *From Here to Eternity: Preparing for the Next Adventure*
and *Experiencing God in Suffering: A Journey with Job*, husband,
father, grandfather, and pastor

My 14 years as a hospice social worker and mental health therapist – and my personal experiences with death – have taught me the significance of accepting the reality of impending death, completing relationships with important people in our lives, and surrendering to the love that is offered to us through Jesus.

In *House Calls With Jesus*, Dr. Lee captures the emotional and spiritual journey her patients face during their dying process. She weaves her own vulnerability and her humanness throughout her patients' stories, exhibiting a role much larger than simply a physician following up on physical symptoms.

Dr. Lee honors her patients' stories in this book just as she clearly honors their personhood during her home visits, offering guidance, encouragement, and comfort to our most vulnerable brothers and sisters. Through giving readers a glimpse of her own faith in action as she ministers to her ailing patients, Dr. Lee portrays a physician concerned with the most important aspect of her patients' healing.

Julie G. Schmidt, LICSW
Pasco, WA, wife, mother, and counselor

In this world, there are few sacred spaces left. However, the space around and surrounding the severely ill and dying is one such space. There is something holy and special that happens when one enters a hospice room, or an ICU, or the bedroom chamber of a terminally ill person. We approach in silence, in reverence, sometimes in fear. For many of us, it is difficult to navigate this space and to know what should be said, what needs to be said, and when to simply be silent and let the space dictate the response. Dr. Jude Lee gives us a glimpse of what it means to engage in these sacred spaces, going on *House Calls with Jesus* and demonstrating for us the deep compassion, grace, and mercy that is required in these places. For anyone who wants to better understand ministry in these kinds of interactions, this book presents windows into the sanctuaries that are found in nursing homes, hospitals, and convalescent rooms all around us. You will be blessed by reading this.

Robert Martin
author *The Caregiver's Beatitudes*, husband, father, software analyst, and blogger at *Abnormal Anabaptist*

House Calls with Jesus is like an old black and white silent movie. Stories shared in silence given life by artistic expression. The beauty of this book is that someone shares what it's like to sit in silence, with compassion and patience listening to the sounds of life so rarely captured in spirit, not word. She then brings those intimate moments alive in her writing with artistic word choice for us to experience them in great detail. In a time when we are all about hustle and bustle and nonstop in doing, someone shows us the lost art of sharing life in stillness. Thank you for the reminder to slow down and be still, and to experience life in our hearts.

Renee Crosby
author *The Fringe* and *Soup Kitchen for the Soul*, wife, mother, and interior designer

HOUSE CALLS WITH JESUS

STORIES OF REDEMPTIVE LOVE

JUDE LEE

Energion Publications
Gonzalez, FL
2016

Sept 2016

Mark —
Your support, prayers and guidance during some great & tough times remains an indelible gift from the Lord through you... in preparation for this and the souls touched by the Lord through this ministry.

Thank you — in Jesus

aka "a" Jude Lee

Copyright © 2016, Jude Lee

Scripture quotations are adapted by the author for use in a conversational setting.

Scriptures marked NKJV are from the New King James Version®. Copyright © 1982 by Thomas Nelson. Used by permission. All rights reserved. Striptures marked KJV are from the King James Version.

Scriptures marked NIV are from THE HOLY BIBLE, NEW INTERNA-TIONAL VERSION®, NIV® Copyright © 1973, 1978, 1984, 2011 by Biblica, Inc.® Used by permission. All rights reserved worldwide.

Scriptures marked RSV are from the Revised Standard Version of the Bible, copyright 1952 [2nd edition, 1971] by the Division of Christian Education of the National Council of the Churches of Christ in the United States of America. Used by permission. All rights reserved.

Scripture quotations marked HCSB are taken from the Holman Christian Standard Bible®, Copyright © 1999, 2000, 2002, 2003, 2009 by Holman Bible Publishers. Used by permission. Holman Christian Standard Bible®, Holman CSB®, and HCSB® are federally registered trademarks of Holman Bible Publishers.

Table of Contents

Introduction

The people who walked in darkness
have seen a great light;
Those who dwelt in the land of the shadow of death,
Upon them a light has shined. Isaiah 9:2, NKJV

These are true stories of a people who have walked, have stumbled, have fallen in their living and in their dying; yet who have tasted and known the goodness of God. Their stories testify to the intimacy God desires with the people He has created. They are testimony to His perfect love which casts out fear and washes over a multitude of sins.

They testify that we have a God who sees, who searches the world over to find men and women whose hearts are willing to be touched by His great grace. It is in these ordinary times, as Jesus is welcomed in, redemptive love has its way, and we become changed people by His presence.

These stories are written to this great God who cares … a testimony to who He is, how He acts in peoples' lives, how He loves us to Himself, and pours out blessing upon blessing. A great light has shined. May you see Him with fresh eyes and fall in love with Him who is Love.

Becoming Bonsai

The day is brilliant, the sun blazing, the air is clear with just a breeze. It soothes a weary soul worn from long traveling through years of struggle and sorrow. Sorrow fills the heart, burdens the feet, invades the warmth of the soul. But in the day to day, it is neatly bundled into a hidden corner. The struggle summons up the energy to take the next step.

Phong, phong, phong. The hollow sound of bamboo rhythmically striking stone measures time. It is slowed to a pace of reverence. The sound of water soothes.

The Japanese garden is the epitome of precision, perfection, and politeness, everything perfect in its place. A soul chaotic in emotion quiets in such order. The simplicity of beauty breathes peace into the core of the heart; the chaos of struggle and sorrow recede to a far place.

Bonsai with stark, bare branches greet the eye: gnarled branches grown into forms of grace and elegant beauty. While deep in thought, a few steps off the ordered path, a place is discovered where many bonsai in transition are scattered about. Wire, raffia lie all over a table. He who is working looks up, startled, sky blue eyes deeply sunk in Californian-tanned handsome blondness, makes a quick glance and returns to the work at hand.

> *Whatta ya' doing?*
> **Wrapping bonsai.**
> *Why?*
> **Making the tree interesting, more beautiful.**
> *Oh, is it hard?*
> **No… Someone comes before me and works with the limbs, making them ready for what is to come.**

Strong tanned hands upon a firm, proud branch: bending, bending, bending, bending. Wire placed, wrap, wrap: bending, bending, bending.

For balance, beauty, in the deep character of this particular tree, a bend is needed right there. It is not in the direction the tree originally intended, nor does it want to go that way, at that time, nor for that long.

Strong tanned hands grip the limb: bending, bending, bending. Sweat begins to trickle, palms wet, breath held: bending, bending, bending the tree. Stretched far beyond its plan, far beyond its comfort, it strains, struggles against the force bending it to a new way of being. Pounding of heart in ears rises, rises, rises:

> It will break, it will break, it will break. Silent
> screams echo in the soul.
> Stop! Stop! Stop!

The exact place is reached and the tree is gently but firmly wrapped against the wire to remain molded where it needs to be. Silence fills the easing tension: breathe in, breathe out. The roar in the ears subsides.

> *How did you know when to stop?*
> **You know because you have worked with the**
> **tree. You know the tree.**
> *What if....? What if...?*
> **I make a mistake? There are graveyards of dead**
> **bonsai.**
> *Graveyards?*
> **Graveyards.**

Brown eyes meet blue.

> *Oh...it is like God working in our lives...*
> **No...   No...**
> **God does not make mistakes.**
> **God does not make mistakes.**

I am the true vine, and
My Father is the vinedresser.
Every branch in Me
That does not bear fruit He takes away;
And every branch that bears fruit
He prunes, that it may bear more fruit.
You are already clean because of the Word
which I have spoken to you.
Abide in Me, and I in you.
As the branch cannot bear fruit of itself,
Unless it abides in the vine,
Neither can you, unless you abide in Me.
I am the vine, you are the branches.
He who abides in Me, and I in him,
Bears much fruit;
For without Me you can do nothing.
For without Me you can do nothing.
  (adapted from John 15:1-5, NKJV)

Deep Calls to Deep

This small house with a sitting porch, a few chairs to watch the road, fields and sky is home to one in her nineties. You can smell the stories as you step out of the car, in the trees, the damp fields, the various remnants of human life scattered amongst the weeds and gravel carport. The "front room" is dimly lit, small, dwarfed by a good-sized man whose voice breaks the reverie of the smell of rain, rotting leaves, and open field.

Ya need some help with that?
No, but thanks.

His hand is big, worn, firm. His sister is quiet, tender tough. Her tiredness pervades her eyes and shoulders. She hesitantly hovers as I prepare to see her mom. Her mom is feisty with a reputation of kicking people out of her room. For one bed bound and having eaten very little for eight weeks, she is sharp and no nonsense. Her previous visitor, the hospice chaplain had asked her how she was. He was greeted with a grunt. To his query, "How many children do you have?" she had retorted, "That is a stupid question, get out!" She is a diminutive wisp of a woman, white hair stark against the nutty, gnarly skin of her face. She has the country style "do" of the South, pulled back, simple bun. She watches me. I stand hesitantly at the threshold of her room. I do not go in.

May I come in to see you? I am Dr. Lee.
Hunh.
I hear tell you are quite a woman. May I come in?
Yes.

Her voice is firm, quiet, filled with authority. I smile, I have met my match. She watches me, eyes sharp, sunk deep in a face of brown wrinkles. Hands thin, so thin with nails curving two inches beyond the weather worn skin that clings to the bones. I lean in, touch her hand.

How are you?
Hunh.

We look at each other. The silence fills the room. Her daughter shifts and speaks:
"Talk to her mom, talk to her. Hey, the doctor is here and she won't talk to her."
The brother appears, concerned.

It's ok, I say to the daughter, turning to her mother again.

We stare at each other. The quiet is warm, her face relaxes.

You must have incredible stories to tell.
I do.
It would be wonderful to hear them.

A grimace, a groan, a wave of nausea distorts her face. It is some time before she is able to compose herself. I ask her about the "spells." She answers, short, concise, to the point.

Well, Mrs. Day, may I take a look at you, check you over?
Ok.

The bedrails are up, creating an uncomfortable barrier to contact, to touch. In the struggle with them, the clanging metal is sharp, stark in this room of stillness. The daughter hovers. The silence builds.

Just going to take your blood pressure.

I lean over, the bed invites me to sit with her tiny frame. The hand on the dial registers her blood pressure, her eyes stare unwaveringly at my face.

Ah, Mrs. Day, you are something. Let me listen to
your heart.

Her hand freed from the blood pressure cuff suddenly moves,
the long nails reach toward my face, the one glancing off my cheek.

Missed your face, she says and settles her open
palm on my cheek.

Her hand is warm, rough, gentle, waiting, on my cheek. I
smile. It stays there as I listen. She slides it to my waist and the
memory of a mother patting her daughter brings tears to my eyes.
Pat, pat, pat, pat. I listen, I touch and brush the wisps of hair from
her face and return the gentle caress to the worn and wrinkled face.
Her eyes close.

She's falling asleep, the doctor's here and she's
falling asleep.
I think she is just resting.   Pat, pat. Pat, pat.

She knows. She hears. She keeps her eyes closed. Her daughter
slips out.

Are you in pain?
No.
Do you have these spells often?
Sometimes.
Would you like me to give you something for them?
Yes.

We "set" then, she and I, and silence joins us, giving space,
and place to be before You, Lord, God, what a space, what a place.

Mrs. Day, I often ask my patients if they would like
me to pray for them. Would you like that? If you
would prefer me not to, well, that would be just fine
also.

Yes, she nods. I take her hand, she closes her eyes and You, O Lord, bathe us in Your love.

> **Thank you,** she murmurs.
> I touch her cheek. *May I come back to see you?*
> **Yes.**

Deep calls to deep in the roar of Your waterfalls.
All Your waves and breakers have swept over me By day,
You, O Lord, direct Your love
At night, Your song is with me.
A prayer to You, O God of my life.
Deep calls to Deep.
(adapted from Psalm 42, NIV)

Jesus, You Know

How are you, sir?

He sits in a wheelchair alone at the edge of the common room, sitting tentatively, shoulders tentative, face tentative, hands, hands held tentatively, poised as if he did not belong. He looks up startled, eyes wide. He has a gentle open face, almost like a deer's face caught in headlights except that there is no fear, not really, just surprise and tentativeness.

How are you, sir? I ask gently again.

Sitting slowly on a nearby low table, I come alongside him and wait. He stares at me a long time. We sit in silence; we are bathed by a quiet tentativeness. I am full of Your Hope, O Lord, and he, he is tentative. He cocks his head:

You know why I am here? He half states, half asks.

I smile, shake my head no. He is surprised. He stares ahead, then away, and pauses a long time. He begins to speak. I can barely hear him. My glance at the unending noise of the huge TV in the corner catches his eye. He quickly goes to turn it off. The movement allows a shifting of position and poise. He settles into his wheelchair more.

I am not accustomed to being listened to. I was a teacher and I listened a lot but ... his voice trails off.
But rarely did anyone listen to you?

He looks at me then full on, eyes intent upon me and nods.

That is right. Where are you from?

We talk a little then about who we are, visitors to the nursing home. He shakes his head.

Nowhere, his head inclines, **where are you from?**
I laugh. *Oh, my background?*

He smiles at my answer. He nods and continues to gaze at us, then he gazes at those around us. I wait gently with him.

You were about to say something?

He nods and remains silent. We wait with him.

Something is on your heart?

He looks up and away. There are no tears in his eyes but I sense them in his heart. The silence of his loneliness fills our space.

Bow down Your ear, O Lord, hear me;
For I am poor and needy. Give ear, O Lord, to my prayer;
And attend to the voice of my supplications.
In the day of my trouble I will call upon You,
For you will answer me.
(adapted from Psalm 86, NIV)

He shakes his head. He whispers:

**I cannot believe you are sitting here waiting to
listen to me.**

We sit in silence then, a long silence, punctuated only by occasional soft sounds beginning in the back of his throat. It is too hard. He struggles, it is too much.

It is too hard right now? I ask.

He nods, trembling.

How 'bout if we pray?

He looks then directly at me, gaze open, heart quiet in stillness and silence. He nods and we pray: Lord, Your Holy Spirit provides the praise and worship and the pleadings of this man's heart. We lift him up in his agony of loneliness, his fear, his sense of abandonment, his grief and loss. We pray Your hope, Your grace, Your love to bring him to You for Your healing mercy. We acknowledge that by Your dying and rising, taking whatever has broken his heart and nailing it to the cross, he is a freed man in You, Jesus, a freed man in You. And Your call upon him is to:

Come, come, ye who are weary and heavy burdened,
And You O Lord will give him rest.
You ask that he take Your yoke upon him
 and learn of You, Jesus.
For You are meek and lowly in heart
And he, he shall find rest for his soul.
Your yoke O Lord is easy.
Your burden is light.
(adapted from Matthew 11:28-30)

At the Amen he gazes long at us, very long and sighs, shakes his head and murmurs:

How did you know? How did you know?
It is Jesus, sir. It is Jesus. He knows.

Your love fills us and he shares his story: of illness, of the loss of his ability to do his work, of taking care of himself, of having to depend on others, of the need to be where he could be taken care of so his daughter would not be so overwhelmed. At the mention of his daughter he whispers:

She will come to see me, won't she? It is not too far to come is it?

We remind him of Your love, of Your sovereignty, of Your grace, of Your answering prayer with mercy and grace in time of need, his need. We remind him how much You love him. He sighs and rests in You. For Jesus, You know. You know.

She Trembles at Your Word

Knock, knock.

I call out as I head down the hallway of this clean, neat house. It is such a contrast to the place where she lived before. The porch on this home is solid concrete; the other was made of shifting boards. This home is dusted and ordered and filled with light; the other, cluttered, chaotic and dark.

She sits on her bed in a blue nylon gown, hair neatly combed and pulled back. I am welcomed into her space. I catch a glimpse of her face right before our eyes meet, before she realizes I can see her, yet am not in her view. The few seconds before someone meets your gaze are precious seconds: people's faces, their expressions are often vulnerably exposed before their "here I am presentable " face settles in. It is during these seconds that the safeguard over deep feeling or conviction is sometimes relaxed; a tiny bit of the person is shared, a precious gift to ponder, to honor.

She is tentative, not sure, almost as if each time she greets someone she is undergoing scrutiny, is being reviewed, is being judged. She seems to expect she will come up wanting; it makes my greeting warm, more welcoming. My delight deepens, as I sense her tension beginning to relax. She is a large woman, a result of having been hurt in spirit, heart and soul to such a point that there was safety and solace in food. Not only has food been comforting but the increased weight protects the sensitive soul within. The beauty of the person is hidden, not exposed, not vulnerable to the onslaught of evil and reproach others often deal out to assuage their own macerated and wounded selves. The protective weight often causes avoidance of one who is thus burdened. The deeper pain of rejection of the inner being, of the sensitive and vulnerable self is temporarily escaped. The expectation of rejection may soften the blow, but the heart still bleeds: drip by drip, tear by tear. Many of these women are sweet, sweet souls, tenderhearted, gentle, willing to meet anyone where they are, willing to go the extra mile, willing to be patient with the other even though they themselves have not been given such a gift. She is such a woman, yet even more.

Her humble and contrite heart grips me. I am reminded of Your words in Isaiah:

> "Has not My hand made all these things and so they came into being?" declares the Lord. "This is the one I esteem: one who is humble and contrite in spirit and trembles at My word." (adapted from Isaiah 66:2, KJV)

She has come into a home filled with blessing. It has given her a hope and deep joy. It has given back a part of her soul where being respected, honored and loved is part of her everyday life. Kind words and acts are not so rare anymore. And she has in turn, become grateful, so grateful and grace-filled.

We talk and tend to that which her physical body needs. I realize she is losing weight. In the encouragement that spontaneously erupts, I sense tears sitting at the threshold of her heart. We talk of her medicines, of small changes that would help her feel better and lessen the burden of her body's suffering. She is so grateful for the smallest effort. I feel unworthy of her gratitude. It is You, Lord, who are working miracles. She catches my eye and tears tremble and fall.

I hope so, she whispers. **This place...**

Her eyes register her room, her home and her heart remembers her family that welcomed her in:

They are so good to me. Jesus has so blessed me. He has given me so much.

Then we must praise Him.

She nods as she gathers my hand into hers. I kneel then before her, the place where I should be, not before her so much, Lord, but before You in her, for the mightiness of Your grace and mercy are so visible. At the calling out of Your name, she trembles. She trembles. My voice falters; the tears well up and my heart overflows with the resonance of both the depth of past sorrow and overflowing joy in this woman. Only in You, Lord, can the depth of sorrow and suffering coexist side by side with deep joy in beauty. We are touched by Your grace. We are overwhelmed by Your mercy. We are brought to our knees in adoration because You are love. You see through our outside selves which are so imperfect, so filled with blunderings and recrimination, so filled with burdens and sorrows that have packed their way around us and around our hearts, sheltering us, providing insulation against future hurt and future love. But in this woman, in this place, in Your presence, light has dawned:

> *You, Lord turn darkness into light.* (2 Samuel 22:29, KJV)
> *You Lord, enlighten our darkness.* (Psalm 18:28, KJV)

> *In You is life, and Your life is the light of men.*
> *And the Light shines in the darkness...*
> *That is the true Light which gives light to everyone.*
> (adapted from John 1: 4-5, 9, NKJV)

Without Your light, without Your love my Lord, our burdens are so heavy, our sufferings ponderously grievous. But You who spoke and said: Let light shine out of darkness (2 Corinthians 4:6, NKJV), made Your light shine in our hearts, made Your light shine in this woman's heart, to give her the light of the knowledge of Your glory, in the face of Christ. You speak to her and say:

> You were once darkness, but now you are light in Me.
> (Ephesians 5:8, NKJV)

> *Live as a child of light, my beloved. Live as a child of light.*

For you are a chosen people, a royal priesthood,
        a holy nation,
A people belonging to Me that you may declare
        My praises.
I have called you out of darkness into My wonderful light.
Once you were not a people but now you are Mine.
Once you had not received mercy
But now you have received mercy.
(adapted from 2 Peter 2:9-10, KJV)

She trembles at Your Word, O Lord, in Your presence. She is humble and contrite in spirit.

Ahhh, dear one, you are becoming so beautiful.

I hug her cheek to cheek. We stay quietly together in Your presence. Her sobs fill our space. Your presence fills our hearts and joy overflows, Lord. Joy overflows.

More Time

Four dead in ten days. Half are prepared.
Half are not.
We want to think there is more time.
More time.
He is thin, very thin, with a face contorting into
tears upon hearing my words:
*I am glad God kept you alive because I had to see
you one more time.*

He is unaccustomed to such words. All his life, he has chosen
the path of being a loner. No deep relationships except a very few.
He has never married. He says he can do with or without people.
He says there is no one that really matters to him. On uttering these
words, his face strains desperately to contain his feelings. When
asked, he says, it is nothing. But it matters I say gently and the tears
well up again. The long silence that follows is not to be interrupted.
He quietly gathers himself, then thanks me for coming. In the same
way, he refuses my offer to pray for him, but he says it is okay that
I pray for him in my car.

So thin, so haggard, so weary: lung cancer with metastasis to
the brain and bone; a diagnosis given less than two months ago.
He has been ill a long time, turning from being tall and thin to
cachectically thin, a concentration camp thinness that is painful
to see. His refusal to see a doctor, to have anything done, speaks
of a subliminal suicide desire. His friend called in hopes we could
convince him to get help.

On that first visit, he sat in the big easy chair, sunk deep in
its soft bowels, his legs bent, long, skeletal before him. Cigarettes
to his left, TV on, the curtains drawn, the room dark and smoky.

He was hesitant to let me into his room. It was a rocky start when he nervously tapped a cigarette and shakily lifted it to his mouth.

Please, please would you not smoke now?

He stopped cigarette mid-air and looked, stunned that after he had already been asked and turned off his TV, now this? No smoking in his own space at this time? Incredible. "What do you think you are?" his face said. His silence was cold, distant. Then he shrugged and placed the cigarette in the ashtray.

It, the shrug, would become his most often said comment. Shrugging off sorrow, worry, faith, relationships, struggle. But deep down inside, it would eat at him much like this cancer was eating, eating, eating him. His only acquiesced concern was pain, physical pain. The rest of his heart was locked away under years of shrugging and silent hurting. He shared little of his past. As a young boy he was always quiet, thin in the background. He was cared for by an aunt, not his own parents. She had died not too long ago. That admission caused a long pause and hesitation. Tears stood at the edge of his thin, sunken eyes and stayed there; they did not fall.

He would share one or two memories or thoughts for each visit. Then, as if having been exposed enough, he would draw into himself and become silent, shrugging through the rest of the conversation.

He almost died. He quit eating suddenly and his friend as steadfast and methodical as he was about most of life; kept right on giving him his blood pressure medicine, his sugar pill, and his pain medicine. On seeing him that day, he was still sitting in the easy chair, sunk back into it. Every now and then, he would jerk, straining to not fall asleep or tip over. He refused to get in the bed. It was easier to sit upright in the chair and rest. A cigarette recently put out was in the ashtray. The room smelled of smoke. It was filled with a stagnant weariness heavier than usual because the man before me could not even shrug.

His blood pressure was barely audible, his pulse thready, his respirations very shallow. I was not sure he was going to make it.

We adjusted medicines and I prayed silently for him. I prayed for him to make it so he would come to know You. The hospice nurse was there and out in the living room; the friend talked and talked. He shared how his friend's illness had affected him, worried him, how much loss he had suffered through recently. Several family members had died in the last month. And then the cat, the cat had been run over by a car. His voice broke. He cried. The tears fell.

He, unlike his friend, shared a lot, his vulnerability achingly visible, his need for comfort openly spoken. We listened, comforted. I asked if I could pray for him and his friend. He offered that it was okay but that was not really something he was ever interested in much. I assured him that we did not have to pray. But he was insistent that I do, giving the impression that it could not hurt and it might help his friend. Might help. Indeed, You answered prayer, Lord, he woke up after twenty-four hours of no medicine.

He now was up and eating. Making it to the bathroom had been critically important and he was able to do that. That day I saw him after his retreat from death's call, he was sitting in the easy chair, legs akimbo, hospital bed nearby with an egg crate mattress upside down. He was very talkative; eyes lit up and he smiled when I exclaimed how great it was to see him up. You are a miracle I said, that you have heartbeat and breath and are sitting there fussing about the mattress. That is a miracle. God must want you here awhile longer. His shrug and smile was one of half acceptance. He talked a lot that visit. He talked of his routine, his day to day activity when he was well. How important it was to get to town after work and hang with his friends, just "easy sharing." His descriptive words about what he did were streetwise, after uttering them, he looked up with eyes a twinkle and apologized. I remarked how good it was to see him smile. How much it mattered that he was alive.

He stopped then mid-thought, his face contorted to tears. They stayed, silent sentinels at the edge of his thin sunken eyes. He seemed more vulnerable this time, unsure about shrugging off his heart. I touched his hand gently. We sat a long time silent. The silence was broken by the sudden appearance of his friend at the bedroom door. We were both startled back to reality. The moment of transparency was shattered. He thanked me for coming, for listening. His gratitude was so sincere, a rare expression of emotion in a man used to not being heard, used to being passed over, used to being overlooked. I patted his hand:

It is a great pleasure sir, a great pleasure to see you,
to be with you.

His eyes filled again. I asked gently:

Can I pray with you this time?

No, he shook his head.

Ok dear, I'll pray for you in the car.

He half-smiled again. I stood up, went to his door and turned.

Sir, it was so good for me to see you. I am so glad
I got to see you again. I had to see you again. I
thought you weren't going to make it last time.
Thank you. I will see you next week.

He nodded, his face contorted to tears. We shook hands and he held my hand a little longer in a firm squeeze. Our eyes locked.

See you then, he nodded.

The rain was coming down. How bereft he is I thought, how alone. How much he needs You, Lord, Your presence, Your comfort, Your strength. Maybe next time, maybe next time.

There is not a next time: he died, two days later.

Let not your hearts be troubled;
You believe in God, believe also in Me.
In My Father's house are many mansions;
if it were not so,
I would have told you.
I go to prepare a place for you.

I will come again and receive you to Myself,
That where I am, there you may be also.
And where I go you know, and the way you know.

Thomas said to Him, "Lord, we do not know
        where You are going,
How can we know the way?"
Jesus said to him, "I am the Way, the Truth, and the Life.
No one comes to the Father except through Me.
No one comes to the Father except through Me.

It is the Spirit who gives life; the flesh profits nothing.
The words that I speak to you are spirit,
        and they are life.
But there are some of you who do not believe.
No one can come to Me unless it has been granted to him
by My Father...
I am the Way, the Truth, the Life.
(adapted from John 14: 1-6; 6:63-65; 14:6, NKJV)

In the beginning was the Word,
And the Word was with God
And the Word was God.
He was with God in the Beginning.
hrough Him all things were made,
Without Him nothing was made that has been made.

In Him was life, and that life was the light of men.
The light shines in the darkness,
But the darkness has not understood it...

He was in the world and though the world
        was made through Him,
The world did not recognize Him.
He came to that which was His own,
but His own did not receive Him.

Yet to all who received Him,
To those who believed in His Name,
He gave the right to become children of God,
Children not born of natural descent,
     nor of human decision
Or a husband's will, but born of God.

The Word became flesh and made His dwelling among us.
We have seen His glory.
The glory of the One and Only Who came from the Fa-
ther,

Full of grace and truth.
Full of grace and truth.
(adapted from John 1:1-14, NIV)

I'm Nuthin' Without Him

The little alley, newly tarred and graveled, is hidden amongst the trees and weeds. The air is hot, the sun bright, a slight breeze makes the heat bearable in the shade. Intent on counting house numbers and seeing none, I keep driving slowly. A little white house of cinder blocks and siding with newly made porch is to my right. I am looking for an apartment in a house, not a house. Inching slowly forward, out of the corner of my eye the image of a country scene in mid-city unfolds.

There is an empty field with wild sweet peas: pink, bright blooms amongst a few trees. It is to the left of another porch on the north side of the little white house. A man sits with sun hat askew, black ringlets of hair peek out from the brim, his black shirt and lavender pants are a striking contrast to the rich brown of his skin. Barely inches away, crocheting with blind eyes, seated in her wheelchair is his wife who had prayed to have a small house with a porch overlooking the mountains where she could sit and be with You, her Jesus. That is how she speaks.

Rhena has known You sometime, Lord. You have been with her since childhood when she was beaten and abused. Surviving through multiple beatings and forced pregnancies, she was left with residual brain damage that resulted in seizures. Shortly after she married Tom, she was hit with a series of seizures that were difficult to control. She had to remain on a ventilator sometime. It was a wonder that she lived, that she continued to have heart and mind alert and capable to love others, to be loved and to proclaim Your love to anyone she could. She was left with residual paraplegia, deafness and near total blindness. Now here she was, in a little house overlooking a field of sweet peas and trees, crocheting.

It is an amazing contrast to the high rise housing development, small one room apartment they had been in. Another Sodom and Gomorrah was Rhena's opinion and she had begun praying to be delivered from such a place that she and her husband were "imprisoned" in. It had been the third move in a year: each move precipitated by eviction or unhappiness with an apartment. The continual call for more from Rhena whether it was better food, more help, mourning what was lost or suspected stolen, and a better place to live created a sense of futility for them both. He was unable to fulfill day to day living needs without great stress and difficulty. It came to a head that day they were evicted with nowhere to go. A decision had to be made to go to the high rise housing development or to put Rhena back in the nursing home and essentially leave Tom to be homeless until he could earn the money to get a new place. That, Lord, precipitated a long conversation of asking Tom if he wanted to answer Your call to him to be spiritual head of house or not. Whether he wanted or was willing to be the one to bring Your Word to his wife, washing her in the water of Your word. We read and prayed Your will. The Scripture You sent, pierced his heart and the heartfelt prayer that followed, asking You to enable him to will and to do according to Your good pleasure, brought him to thoughtful silence and tears.

By Your providence, they ended up at the high rise housing development. There many good things happened: Tom grew in You, giving rise to diligent care of his wife both physically and spiritually. He began to make efforts to lose weight, to accept the need to pay off old bills that had been keeping them in bad credit. Your Word was handwritten out in large script for Rhena to read. His music blossomed in You Lord and blessed many.

A series of semi-conscious spells of "jerking all over" prompted hospitalization for Rhena. Her description starkly differed from the medical opinion of uncontrolled seizures: spirits of evil and fear fought over her, prompting visions of struggle deep within, causing her to grow wide-eyed with fear and "jerking all over." In the middle of that, she called out to You, Your Spirit came upon her powerfully, washing her clean, filling her with a sweet anointing. She woke, calling out to her husband to read Your Word. Though she could not hear the words, Your Word penetrated her heart and she was transformed. She rose from her miry pit of covetousness, self-worry and fear and became a woman filled up with joy in Your presence. Your preeminence radiating through her eyes and face, the jerking stopped, the sweet breath of Your Holy Spirit wafting in her, enabled her to see and be in a way never before.

A way opened up by Your holy timing for them to rent a little house with porch and yard: a worldly impossibility in view of their past and little income. But there is nothing too hard for You Lord: NOTHING! You delivered them out of their trial into the presence of peace, Your peace.

On touching her arm as I arrive on the porch, Rhena turns and her full face crinkles with joy. Her eyes open wide and she speaks words she did not know before Your Holy Spirit brought her to Your transforming presence:

The Lord is my shepherd,
I shall not want.

Her chest vibrates with the depth of conviction in her heart. The words strong are sent out with purpose:

He maketh me to lie down in green pastures:
He leadeth me beside the still waters.
He restoreth my soul:
He leadeth me in the paths of righteousness for His
Name's sake.
Yea, though I walk through the valley
    of the shadow of death,
I will fear no evil; For Thou art with me;
Thy rod and Thy staff they comfort me.

Thou preparest a table before me
    in the presence of my enemies:
Thou anointest my head with oil; My cup runneth over.
Surely goodness and mercy shall follow me

all the days of my life:
And I will dwell in the house of the Lord forever.
(Psalm 23, KJV)

The birds and breeze echo praise; Your Spirit moves again. She intones in a deep, rich full voice:

Let not your heart be troubled: ye believe in God,
      believe also in Me.
In My Father's house are many mansions:
      if it were not so,
I would have told you. I go to prepare a place for you.
And if I go and prepare a place for you,
I will come again and receive you unto Myself;
That where I am, there ye may be also.
And whither I go ye know, and the way ye know.

Thomas saith unto Him, Lord, we know not
      whither Thou goest;
And how can we know the way?
Jesus saith unto him, I am the way, the truth
      and the life:
No man cometh unto the Father but by me.
(adapted from John 19:1-6, KJV)

Your presence and Your Word bring us to reverential silence. Standing near, I squeeze her shoulder and praise You silently. Her right hand rises slowly and moves in adoration of You, Jesus. Tears roll down her broad sweet face. She closes her eyes, sees You and speaks Your Name. You bless us with breeze and time of silent worship and praise. She queries:

Dr. Lee, you know what Jesus is a teachin' me?
No, Rhena, tell me.
He's a teachin' me I am nuthin', without Him.
Without Jesus, we're nuthin'.
Without Him, we're nuthin'.
He's a openin' a ministry for me.
I can feel He's a openin' a way. He's a brought

me this far, ain't nuthin' goin' make me go back.

Nuthin' can be a stoppin' Jesus.

Nuthin' can be getting' between me and Jesus.

You Lord Jesus say:

I am the way, the truth and the life. (John 14:6, KJV)

I am the door of the sheep:
I am come that they might have life
and that they might have it abundantly.
I am the good Shepherd:
The good Shepherd giveth His life for the sheep.
I am the good Shepherd, and know my sheep,
And am known of mine.
As the Father knoweth Me, even so know I the Father:
And I lay down my life for the sheep.
(adapted from John 10:7b, 10b, 15, KJV)

I am the vine, ye are the branches
He that abideth in Me, and I in him,
the same bringeth forth much fruit;
for without Me ye can do nothing.
(John 15:5, KJV)

Frail Beauty of Life

The delight of this little one just to be, brings my heart bowing before You. She glows with Your love and laughter. She delights in the sweet little things of life: the sound of Velcro opening and closing, paper moved by a tiny hand contracted into permanent flexion at the knuckle, the small open fist hits the adjacent wall gently: thud, thud. She erupts into peals of open laughter which shakes her whole being, shakes this little one who has had cerebral palsy all her forty some years. Her eyes, blue gray, roam separately, never quite focusing but searching, searching to see what is before her. At any unexpected sound or gentle touch, she crinkles into delight and laughter.

It is the glow of her clear pink face against a shirt of purple stripes and matching purple bands in her pigtails that rivets me, making me wonder in whose presence I have come. You Lord, abide and shine forth in her, she is unfettered by the complications of a mind that seeks to do. Being comes naturally to her, she welcomes being still and knowing You Jesus, in a way that we who "do" so busily cannot fully appreciate.

As I stand and touch her cheek ever so gently and call her name, the faces, names and cries of the wounded and dead from the recent massacre rise up. The sacred safety of this little place, this little home filled with Your love brings me to weeping. Where are they, Lord? Do they, did they, know You? How are they making it, those left behind? Do they have You to be their comfort and peace? It takes Your strong hand to uphold hearts so bereft at such a time as this..

She has learned when there is pressure on her arm, a needle stick may follow. In my touch and voice, she senses any tension or anxiety. With great effort, Lord, I bring the trembling within, for You to still and to guide. It is the Velcro opening of the blood pressure cuff that disrupts the quiet tension that has momentarily filled the room. It is enough to settle us to enjoy her spontaneous delighted laughter. The visit continues as is usual until prayer.

How is it Lord, whenever people who have any illness that prevents the normal function of mind or speech, the question: "Want to pray to the Lord?" rivets their attention. At Your name, at the mention of talking with You, hearts still, fluttering and noise quiet; sometimes there is a clear, "of course" or "yes, thank you" when the babbling just seconds before makes no sense, except to You.

It is this same way, O God, when we come to You with whatever state our heart is in, Your Holy Spirit moves words to pour forth from Your Word:

> *Father, You find us in a desert land*
> *And in the howling waste of wilderness, You encircle us,*
> *You come for us,*
> *You keep us as the apple of Your eye.*
> (adapted from Deuteronomy 32:10, RSV)

> *Anyone who touches Your children,*
> *Touches the apple of Your eye.*
> (Zechariah 2:8, RSV)

> *The sorrows of death compassed me,*
> *The floods of ungodly men made me afraid,*
> *The sorrows of hell compassed me about,*
> *The snares of death confronted me.*

> *In my distress I called upon You Lord,*
> *And cried to You my God:*
> *You heard my voice out of Your temple*
> *And my cry came before You, even into Your ears.*
> *Then the earth shook and trembled,*
> *The foundations also of the hills moved*
> *And were shaken because You were filled with wrath.*

There went up a smoke out of Your nostrils and
Fire out of Your mouth devoured:
    Coals were kindled by it.
You bowed the heavens and came down and
Darkness was under Your feet.
    And You rode upon a cherub and
Did fly, yea, You did fly upon the wings of the wind.

You made darkness Your secret place,
Your pavilion round about You were dark waters
    and thick clouds of the skies.
At the brightness before You, Your thick clouds passed,
Hailstones and coals of fire. You Lord,
    thundered in the heavens,
And You, the Highest gave Your voice: hailstones
    and coals of fire.
Yea, You sent out Your arrows and scattered them and
You shot out lightning and discomfited them.

Then the channels of waters were seen and
The foundations of the world were discovered
    at Your rebuke,
O Lord, at the blast of the breath of Your nostrils.
You send from above, You took me; You drew me
    out of many waters.
You delivered me from my strong enemy,
    and from them which hated me:
For they were too strong for me. They confronted me in
the day of my calamity
But You Lord were my stay, You brought me forth also
into a large place;
You delivered me because You delight in me.
(adapted from Psalm 18:4-19, KJV)

Where is that large place Lord, You have delivered to? You have delivered from an enemy that is too strong, an enemy that has brought calamity into lives this day, a strong enemy that hates. But Lord, You are my stay. When we see people falling and crying out and calamity has come upon us, death is all around: what do these words mean O God who saves? Our hearts screams against the senselessness of such vile hate and destruction, against the heart-break of lives so cared for brought to death. And it is then Your Son speaks:

> *My God, My God, why have You forsaken Me?*
> (Matthew 27:45, NKJV)

Your Son is hanging with the weight of death, the weight of all the sin of all humanity upon Him: massacre after massacre, tortured victim after tortured victim, abused child after abused child, destruction of life, destruction of relationship, destruction of family, lust, greed, covetousness, pride, arrogance, and vile thing after vile thing upon Him, Your Only Son. Our humanity is filled up with unspeakable evil perpetuating itself over and over because we love the darkness and do not want to give over to You who are Light and Love.

You have taken it all and in the middle of such an enemy of death, destruction and evil, You died. You died for us, bearing all the evil of the world. You, perfect, without any evil, without any sin, dying. God, Your Father, did not spare You, did not spare You but gave You, His only Son to suffer, to die for us. If there is any other way, You had asked Your Father in the garden: "Not My will but Yours, be done… (Luke 22:42, NKJV)." And You seeing the joy set before You, endured the cross, despising the shame (Hebrews 12:2, KJV).

There was no other way to pay the penalty for such evil. You, died and suffered but on the third day You rose. You rose, having defeated death, destruction, and evil not by death of death or death of destruction or death of evil but by freeing us Your children from being bound—slaves to death, destruction and evil so that in life we can live abundantly; in physical death, we can be alive forever in You. Even in our physical dying, You bring us to a place, a large place. You tell us where that is in Psalm 118:

You bid us enter in Your gate
Enter in to righteousness,
Enter in to You,
Enter in to salvation,
Enter in to Your doing where it is marvelous in our eyes.
Enter into the day You have made:
A day of rejoicing and gladness,
A day of blessing and joying in You.
Enter in to You O Lord: You are good.
Enter in to You O Lord: You are mercy,
Enter in to You O Lord: You endure forever.
You are our large and broad place in which we stand.
We will not fear.
(adapted from Psalm 118, NKJV)

You, Lord our God in the midst of us are mighty.
You save, You rejoice over us with joy,
You rest in Your love, You joy over us with singing.
(adapted from Zephaniah 3:17, KJV)

Keep our eyes upon You Lord in the day of our calamity that we might see You who are mighty to save: see You in the midst of death, in the midst of sorrow and agonizing suffering. Hold us Lord, bring us to life in You. Thank You that in our physical dying or living we, Your children, can be with You. Find us Lord in that desert place, in that howling waste of wilderness, encircle us, come for us, keep us as the apple of Your eye.

She delights in You Lord, her laughter rings out and she trembles at touch and prayer and quiets. At the mention of her loving You, O Lord, she speaks words all run together, but the heart understands them: I love Him, I love Him. And in Your great love, Jesus, You envelope us. We weep in sorrow, in gratitude for the frail beauty of life. We rejoice in You, the Giver of Life. Hold us Lord; we are unable without You in this world.

In memory of those who fell at Virginia Tech on April 16, 2007 and a wee one who did not know and laughed delightedly in You, Lord ... because You are good.

Magnify the Lord

It is a sunny day with a breeze that is crisp and dry; there are only a few high clouds. The air is clean: it is like a fall day in May, a glorious day. To see the last patient of the day requires a trek up the long ramp: rap, rap at the door. The knock at the door signals a stepping into the time and space of the one being seen. A doctor's time does not exist in this realm: everything swings into the pace, place and personhood of the one being visited. How quickly someone comes to the door is poorly estimated for shuffling gait or wheelchair maneuvering can hinder prompt response. Any restriction of hearing may mean the rapping goes unheard or is mistaken for part of the background noise of the TV or neighborhood. To rap or ring again is always a testimony to the heart's willingness to be patient; on some days, it is easier than others. It is a short delay. The door swings open.

Come in.

The screen door clangs shut; he closes the door. It is dark with the drapes drawn. The blue sky vanishes. With a quick, deft hand, he backs his wheelchair back and to the right, forward and to the right again and settles indicating with his head that my usual place on the couch is ready. I sag into the seat at the edge. He, a big man fills the chair; his right side is straight and fully operational; his left lies limp, hand swollen from hanging and inactivity. Both feet are flat on the floor and move like silent sentinels in felt slippers to and fro whenever the chair is moved. Click, click…slide, slide… it is the sound of dexterity in practice. For his seventy some years, he has adapted, surviving the stroke. His hope, his only hope has been to walk again and get a job.

Get a job? Doing what?

**Working with my hands. Making something
for Jesus.**

We have had a routine of sorts: getting a short medical history of his past month followed by washing my hands in the dark, at the sink of his kitchen that has a black green floor, then back to the living room where his blood pressure is checked, his heart, lungs and legs are examined and his medications are reviewed. We would then talk of what God was doing in his life. At the signal of ending, I would ask:

Can I pray for you?
Ah…he would say with a satisfied sigh; **that is
what I am waiting for.**

Over many intervening months stretching into a couple of years, it was hard to see the lack of progress, the increasing weakness and the difficulty to keep skin integrity intact. All these signs began to herald a possible move to a nursing home. It came one day when change was inevitable. The decubiti he had nursed silently suddenly became deep and tunneling. His stay at the hospital was long and arduous. It was months before a call came from him requesting to be seen again.

At arrival at his home, a different car in the driveway hints of change. Up the long ramp, knock, knock at the door: the quick footsteps in response are a surprise. The door opens; the sunshine of that day floods in and remains. A woman, tall, thin, stern in demeanor and proud steps back. The place and the man are transformed: the clutter is gone, sunlight fills the room; the stale air of stuck routine is gone. He is thinner, healthier appearing, moving swiftly in a motorized wheelchair with that amazing dexterity he had before but so much darkness is shed from the walls, the windows, the door and the floor, and him. The kitchen is flooded with light and the floor, the kitchen floor is a brilliant chartreuse and yellow.

Oh my…has it always been this color?

The woman's response reflects her pride; a small delighted smile eases the tension of the newness in the visit. A song of praise rises up and is shared silently with You Lord as hands are washed:

Strength will rise as we wait upon the Lord,
We will wait upon the Lord,
We will wait upon the Lord.

Our God, You reign forever
Our hope, Our strong deliverer.
You are the everlasting God,
The everlasting God,
You do not faint, You won't grow weary.

You're the defender of the weak,
You comfort those in need,
You lift us up on wings like eagles.
(from Everlasting God by Chris Tomlin)

The physical exam reveals a man filled up with renewed hope and spirit. By divine intervention, a near death experience for his wife brought the two of them back together at the time of his stay in the nursing home. Her relationship with You Lord is ecstatic, full, filled up with steadfast determination and clinging to You for all things. A corner of the house is reserved and beautified simply to be with You in Your Word. There is evident testimony to Your bountiful giving to receptive hearts in love with You. The green of the living plants, the multitude of colorful fish in tanks are such a delight. There is joy in the heart of the man who is determined to walk with You, expecting You, Lord, to pave the way for Your will to be done: he is energized, filled up with Your Spirit.

Amazing, amazing. You are amazing, I say to him.
You are amazing, I say to her.
Our God is amazing. Our God is amazing.

We all smile and laugh and praise You.

Let's pray.

Now that's what I've been waitin' for.

We will bless You Lord at all times.
Your praise shall continually be in our mouth.
Our souls shall make our boast in You Lord:
The humble shall hear and be glad.

O magnify the LORD with us,
Let us exalt His name together.
We sought You Lord, You heard us,
You deliver us from all our fears.

We look to You and are radiant,
Our faces are not ashamed.
We who are poor cry out and You LORD hear us.
You hear and save us out of all our troubles.
Your angel O LORD encamps round about us
That fear You and You deliver us.

O taste and see that the Lord is good:
Blessed is the man that trusts in You.
Blessed is the woman that trusts in You.
Blessed are we Lord who trust in You.
(adapted from Psalm 34:1-8, NKJV)

Remember Who You Are

She is a small woman whose color is magenta, whose suffering is grievous, whose losses are great and she cries:

Thank You, Jesus. Thank You, Jesus.

Tears stream down her face, her right arm is pierced by pain. She, a woman of stately bearing and elegant features has already suffered a paralysis of one side of her body; she cannot fully express herself due to the hemorrhagic stroke that struck her when she was so young. Words of anguish and sorrow, words of grace and peace, words of care and love have been minimized to only a few. This compounds the suffering. She cries out and I weep silently and cry out for her. The words in my heart remain unspoken:

> *O my God, my God why have You allowed this? I am mad. I am so upset. I am torn by her suffering and now this? More pain, more bone pain causing her to writhe in agony with an unbearable wailing because the pain is so intense. Lord God have mercy...what are You doing? Lord God have mercy... please stop the suffering.*
> *Lord God have mercy...please this way of love is too hard. Lord God have mercy.*

I whisper to her:

> *Don't forget who you are.*

She looks at me hard with her eyes, dark, deep in their suffering. Her silence fills me.

> *Don't forget who you are, You are royalty.*
> *You are daughter of the Most High God,*

King of all Creation. You are His.
You are a royal priesthood. You are a Holy nation.
You are a beloved of His and He delights in you.

Her dark eyes fill up at the remembrance of Your call upon her. She shudders and shakes violently in her weeping, receiving Your embrace, being filled up with Your love.

Don't forget who you are.

The words falter and break. I am unable Lord, and we weep together in her agony borne by You Lord, borne by You.

Blessed is this woman for her delight is in You,
        her delight is in Your law;
Her meditation on Your Word fills her up day and night.
She is like a tree planted by the rivers of water
That bring forth its fruit in its season,
Whose leaf also shall not wither
        and whatever she does shall prosper.
(adapted from Psalm 1, NKJV)

        Blessed is this woman who trusts in You
Lord and whose hope is You.
For she shall be like a tree planted by the waters,
Which spreads its roots by the river
        and will not fear when heat comes;
But its leaf will be green
        and will not be anxious in the year of drought
nor will cease from yielding fruit.
(adapted from Jeremiah 17:7-8, NKJV)

Blessed are we, O Lord. At Your first use of "blessed" in Scripture You tell us of Your creating living creatures. You do not bless the heavens or the earth or the light or the darkness: Nor the seas, nor the grass, the fruit trees, or the herb that yield seed, nor the greater light that rules the day, nor the lesser light that rules the night, nor the multitude of stars. But when You, O Lord, created living creatures, You blessed them saying:

*Be fruitful and multiply, fill the waters in the seas and
let birds multiply on the earth.*
(adapted from Genesis 1:22, KJV)

*And when You Lord created man in Your own image,
      according to Your likeness:
male and female You created them.*
(adapted from Genesis 1:27, KJV)

You blessed them saying:

*Be fruitful and multiply, fill the earth and subdue it.
Have dominion over the fish of the sea,
      over the birds of the air
And over every living thing that moves on the earth.*
(adapted from Genesis 1:28, KJV)

You alone the Creator can bless and give life. In Your blessing, growth begins, a deep planting to receive what is needed to bear fruit, fruit that magnifies Your glory, filling up the earth with Your Holiness, Your beauty, and wonder of You, Lord God. In the middle of fruitfulness, in the middle of growth, in the middle of life at its prime, one is stricken. Our world is beset with brokenness, a terrible un-wellness since the fall in the Garden of Eden. It eats at every living thing. In its hunger to devour what You have created, it seeks to suck life and hope, worship and adoration from You. It seeks to mock and scorn You, the Creator. There but by Your grace we walk with You. The line between the ungodly: those who refuse to hear Your call of love or who run from receiving Your goodness and those who are like the tree planted by the river of waters, is just a simple turning.

Your Word in Isaiah tells us how far Your people have gone from You and in their choosing the wrong path, refusing to hear Your call of love, their hearts are hardened, they cannot see or hear or understand You or they would have turned, they would have turned to be healed by You (Isaiah 6:9-10). But there are many who love You Lord, who do not escape the calamity and destruction of this present world's darkness, whose lives are shattered and broken. There is no good explanation for their suffering and I struggle and chafe and cry out to You in anguish for their pain. Your beaten, tormented body and face remind us that You have borne all pain, all suffering, all agony, all torment, all illnesses, all destruction, all the wailing of each and every human on the face of the earth from the beginning of time to now and future. You have borne it in silence as a lamb led to slaughter and by Your wounds we are healed, by Your wounds we are healed. (*adapted from* Isaiah 53:5, NIV)

Ah, sweet lady whose color is magenta, whose tears flow continuously from your heart. Can you see the Lord? He is here. He holds you. He has borne your sorrow and is bearing it still. He calls you His own. You are His beloved.

> *He rejoices over you with gladness.*
> *He quiets you with His love.*
> *He rejoices over you with singing.*
> (adapted from Zephaniah 3:17, NKJV)

> *Do not fear: Though the fig tree may not blossom,*
> *Nor fruit be on the vines,*
> *Though the labor of the olive may fail and*
> *The fields yield no food;*
> *Though the flock may be cut off from the fold and there*
> *be no herd in the stalls...*
> *Yet will you rejoice in the LORD? Will you joy in the God*
> *of your salvation?*
> (adapted from Habakkuk 3:17-18, NKJV)

Remember who you are. You are His beloved daughter, woman after His own heart in whom He delights...the apple of His eye.

> *Rejoice in the Lord.*
> *Joy in the God of Your salvation,*
> *For He is your strength.*
> *He makes your feet like deer feet*
> *He will make you walk on the high hills.*
> (adapted from Habakkuk 3:17-19, NKJV)

Your Beloved speaks. He who suffered for you, He who died for you, He speaks:

> *Rise up, My love, My fair one and come away.*
> *For lo, the winter is past,*
> *The rain is over and gone,*
> *The flowers appear on the earth;*
> *The time of singing has come,*
> *And the voice of the turtledove is heard in our land.*
> *The fig tree puts forth her green figs*
> *And the vines with the tender grapes give a good smell.*
> *Rise up My love, My fair one and come away!*
> (adapted from Song of Solomon 2:10-13, NKJV)

It is Well with My Soul

The horror and desperation in her voice resonate with the pounding of my heart as I go up the stairs: by the second step, the smell, the permeating smell of flesh failing gives me a desire to flee. But You, Lord, stay me. You are my stay.

A wound dressing change, done without consultation, has unintentionally caused a grievous horror. Our hearts cry out in rebellion against the way all flesh goes. The wound folded upon itself had wept, with the weeping: it rotted. The removal of the bandage released the collection of fleshly tears and portions of tissue that were no longer. Gaping holes where none should be, brought my heart to my knees. In the first attempt to clean, to wash gently, the flesh falls, the bones are exposed.

Lord...

She moans. It is the image of this frail lady feisty in heart, in spirit, beautiful in her well-tended care, plaited hair, matching pajamas, robe and quilt gracing her long legs in Your presence, Lord, that gives the impetus to do what needs to be done. Your strength Lord, stays me.

In Psalm 65:2, You tell us Lord, all flesh shall come to You... all flesh. Until now, what I had seen on the cross, on You Lord was sin in flesh and blood, flesh in the horror of violence and blood and gore, suffering and agony. But life in a clean world of refrigeration, air-conditioning, antiseptics, death contained in white sheets, antiseptic smelling morgues and scenes on TV are not fully the face of sin. Sin is putrid, rotting, pervasive, pernicious in its never-ending quest for more flesh to devour and rot.

But Lord Jesus, You say: Unto You all flesh comes: all sin, all evil, all flesh. The price You have paid, none can fathom. But it is at Your cross Lord, we need to be reminded again and again Lord:

Out of You comes the river of life, waters abundant without end, never, never running out, cleansing, cleansing away sin and rot. You are victorious Lord over sin and death: all sin, all death, all evil, all rot. You have redeemed each and every human on the face of the earth: bought, paid for, and delivered from slavery to rot. You are light and in You, Lord, there is no darkness at all. There is no darkness at all.

Happy in Jesus

There is one who knows You Jesus, who has walked with You long yielded to Your love. She knows the truth of Your loving. At her door this day, there is no answer. After several more knocks, my heart quiets when I hear the electric release which signals the opening of the door. I walk in and lock eyes with her.

I am so weak.

Her head languishes on the back of her chair. She gazes at me quietly. There is still fire in her eyes but they are embers gently glowing, not the fast, dancing fire of previous years, of recent previous days. Her skin so alive before holding her firmly on this earth is thin, limp with multiple folds upon itself, reminding me that once upon a time this lady struggled with her weight. Her skin has a yellow green cast. The weight of the air and acknowledging weakness is hard for this lady who adamantly will not give up; it signals an understanding that You, Lord, do have Your way in her. She knows You. She sighs as she looks out her window. The flowers and newly budding trees beckon, praise You with their arms and faces uplifted to You in adoration.

She would so often say: I am so blessed. I am so blessed. These words were vibrant testimony in the midst of her aloneness, to her sometimes confined life of sitting in chair, crocheting, praying to You. Now, the added weakness makes her very still. It is out of character for her: she was a woman who would move from chair to kitchen with her walker as if she had rocket fuel in her feet. Her hands which were so busy before shaping her words in the air lie still.

We go through a slow check but it is clear: there is no manipulation of medicine that will make a difference here. She knows it and does not show emotion when I recommend she needs to have someone with her whenever she gets up.

> *You are so weak, my dear. I am afraid you will fall.*
> *You have already fallen last week.*
> **I don't know how that will work out,** she murmurs.
> *Yes, it will take some talking over to see what your options are.*

She is quiet. We both do not speak the obvious. I study her face. She is one whose main emotion is thanksgiving and joy. She would rarely cry: if she did, after a short release of tears she would say: Okay, enough. We must smile. Lord, You are so good to me and with a sigh of thanksgiving she would shake herself and allow You to lift her head.

She looks at me. I slide off the couch to kneel before her. I gather her hands into mine and hold them, hold them, hold her hands which so many times held mine in vigorous grip:

> *Tell me what you are thinking dear.*
> **I don't want to tell you.**
> *Oh…* I say.

The silence fills the room. It is many sighs and breaths later, she whispers:

> **I like it here.**
> *Yes, I can see that.*
> **I don't want to go to a nursing home; I don't think I will do very well.**

Her voice trails off. We both take a slow breath in and she weary-worn, rests her head on my shoulder. I release her hands and hold the shoulders that used to be so busy and full. Her bones meet my grieving hands; we are brought before Your altar in tears.

It is not easy Lord, this dying to self. It is not easy. We wait at the altar in silence, in reverence of the work of sacrifice and love:

Your sacrifice, Your love which envelops her and her willingness to be living sacrifice unto Your glory, unto the praising and joying in You. You fill us with Your presence. Your peace comes, Your comfort surrounds and strengthens, bringing a movement ever so slight in her frame. She pulls back and looks me in the eye:

Whatever He wants, she says firmly,
I am happy.
I am happy. I have Jesus. I am happy.
I am so happy.

She beams through her tears, radiant beyond words. We grasp hands again and in Your Spirit we are led to pray in You, to praise You, to call upon You for guidance, help and blessing, for Your paving the way to Your will and giving thanks for walking with her and all whom she loves through the valley of the shadow of death. You are with her O Lord, You are with her. Your rod and Your staff are her comfort. You set a table richly filled before her in the presence of her enemies of illness and fear. You anoint her head with oil. She is Your beloved daughter. You Who are King of kings and Lord of lords, the Creator of the universe, sustain all by Your holy will, You are her Father; You Jesus love her. You love her. Fill her Lord with Your goodness and mercy all the days of her life that she may dwell with You Lord in Your presence forever and ever. She sighs into my ear. During prayer her need for resting in You comes upon her. I remind her again of the need to only be up when someone is with her. She nods and says in my ear:

I've been so afraid of falling, so afraid. It's a
bad feeling.

With a breath of thanks, she rests again on my shoulder. I hold her tightly and we weep together in You.

Thank You, Lord, for loving this little lady. Thank
You, Lord, for the blessing of her life.

Thank You, Lord, for carrying her all the way to You.
(adapted from Psalm 63:1-7)

You brought her home to You, Lord, on Easter
morn.

A Light Note

Answering service, voice a bit frantic: 'Mrs. Key says Mr. Key has just died."

> *Mrs. Key, hello.*
> **Oh hello, doctor.**
> *What happened?*
> **I think he just passed away.**
> *Are you sure? How can you tell?*
> **When I lift his arm and let it drop, it just drops.**
> *He does not respond to you in anyway?*
> **No…it's sad isn't it?**

I am gathering my thoughts. O Lord, how to respond over the phone? A sound escapes my throat, no real word, just a sound.

> **Oh, are you crying?**
> Silence. What to say?
> *Uh no, I was thinking of you.*
> **It's really too bad isn't it? My sister just died last week.**
> *Oh, I thought it was several weeks ago.*
> **No.**
> *That is really hard.*
> **We had a really good day yesterday, and we had a good day today.**
> **I was just not expecting it to be today. It is really sad, isn't it? Oh, the EMTs have arrived.**

Noise on the phone.

> **Oh, he just opened his eyes!**

He just opened his eyes?
Oh, yes!!! Bye...

Behold What Manner of Love

He lives in the back room next to the window that overlooks the porch. He is a large man, the room is small, neat. Another single bed with a white spread is neatly made beside his. He is unable to say much, unable to move his right side due to a stroke. His ADLs, Activities of Daily Living, are all taken care of by his wife. She has been doing this for years. Up until 6 months ago, he had been able to get up and stand on his good leg and pivot into a wheelchair.

Increasing problems with recurrent pneumonia, little strokes and sepsis have weakened him. These last six months have been hard confining her to full care and him to the four walls of this small room. We spoke of a Hoyer lift. After several weeks of hesitation, she got brave enough to use it and attain her hope that he would be able to sit on the front porch with her and enjoy the day.

They were late bloomers in You, Lord, having come to know You after they had the one child, perhaps even after she had left and had been gone for so long. Their love for You is deep and abiding, a joy that resonates deep in their souls. Delight in You spreads across their faces, transforming fatigue into radiance, sad faces into peace-filled countenances that emanate Your warmth and Your love. It is a love born and bred out of deep sorrow.

The one thing that has gripped my heart is how he loves her with his eyes. He cannot articulate his feelings beyond an "awwww" the way one would say it before a slow "aw shucks". It is an "awwww" filled with gentle regret that is drawn out with that Southern languid desire of wanting it to be otherwise. He would turn his head to his right side where she would almost always be and then love her, love her with his eyes. Not just briefly but long, long and lovingly. At times I was embarrassed I was in the room because their love was so unabashed, so unashamed, so intense. Sensuality was not overtly there but the deep resonance of the love bespoke a Love that embodied fully mind, heart, spirit and body. It was intense, warm and full.

> **He is my whole life. I know he is dying, why**
> **can't they leave me alone with him and not talk**
> **to me about death.**

She is angry. Tears rise up; she wrings her hands. Her gentle way of acceptance stiffens into rebellion, ready to battle anyone or thing that would threaten to take him from her.

> **Why do they tell me to tell him it is okay for**
> **him to go? It is not okay for him to go. I don't**
> **want him to go.**

Her cry rises to a pitch. My body is shaken by her anguish and I remember his look of love. She collapses inward then, her face, her shoulders crumble and I hold her. Her sobs shake her and me. Her tears drop on my shoulder and mine strain to turn into deep sobs. Her pain is touching a deep buried pain of my own and I cannot let the door loose upon it. She needs You Lord in her sorrow, not me in mine.

Thank You, Lord for catching every tear. Thank You, O Lord for hearing every cry. Thank You, Lord for bearing up against all our anger. Thank You, Lord for loving us so intensely.

We share prayer then after a long, long cry. It is the only way to bring temporary closure to such sorrow. We pray for Your holy timing, Your holy wisdom, Your loving presence to hold her, to guide her to knowing when to let go, to know in her heart what her beloved husband would want and how he needs to know she will be okay. He had always taken care of her; she has cared for him so completely these last years. Now he must transfer his responsibility fully to You Lord. And she will need to rest totally in You.

We go into him, to share prayer. I wonder if it is my last time to see him. He cannot stay awake during the whole prayer but smiles broadly after we finish. I cross to his right side and he turns his eyes to me and loves me. His left arm reaches over and hugs me deeply to his face. His gaze penetrates my soul and I know Your love through him has reached a tender guarded place. We stare at each other recognizing it might be in a different place that we might meet again. She calls out:

I haven't had one of those in awhile.

Our laughter mixes with the well of sorrow and before I reach the front door, the tears are cascading onto the carpet. I escape to the car, letting the sobs find their release: a grief that has remained hidden a long time has been touched by Your gentle hand. I am reminded how much it hurts to love deeply.

Your Son, Your Only Son, Your Beloved Son, suffering pain, sorrow, unspeakable agony, yet, You love still. You Lord love still, with all Your being. Will we, will we?

Behold what manner of love the Father has given
  unto us,
that we should be called the sons of God,
that we should be called the sons of God.
(adapted 1 John 3:1a, KJV)

And this is His commandment that we should believe on
the name of His Son Jesus Christ and love one another.
(1 John 3:23, KJV)

Redeemed from Dust

In walking with the Lord day by day, we are called to respond to Him, to His call. As we yearn to hear Him, to hear His will, our desire is to glorify Him, to honor Him. But sometimes, the unexpected or unwanted happens. We do not see it coming nor do we seem prepared. Loss brings us to our knees; we have seen the hope of our hearts or the work of our hands fall before us.

The story of the Shunammite woman in 2 Kings 4:8-37 speaks to such loss and the response of one in touch with God. The woman of Shunem is a "notable woman (NKJV)," a woman who welcomed Elisha persuading him to eat in her home. She and her husband, who was said to be old, had no children; yet there was no bitterness in her that would prevent offering hospitality. They prepared a place of rest and nourishment for Elisha in his regular travels through Shunem. Elisha desired to do something for her for all the trouble she took for him, yet there appeared to be nothing she needed; she was content in her life amongst her people. This puzzled Elisha, so he asked:

> "Then what should be done for her?"
> Gehazi (his servant) answered, "Well, she has no son and her husband is old."
> "Call her," Elisha said. So Gehazi called her and she stood in the doorway. Elisha said, "At this time next year you will have a son in your arms."
> And she said, "No, my lord. Man of God, do not deceive your servant!"
> But the woman conceived and gave birth to a son at the same time the following year, as Elisha had promised her. (2 Kings 4:14-17, HCSB)

It can only be imagined what kind of mother this woman of Shunem was, having been surprised by the gift of a son which she did not expect. What a delight, what a joy she must have had in him. In the midst of an ordinary day, her hope and joy began to unravel. The child had gone out to his father who was with the reapers early one morning and he was stricken in the field with an illness which made him cry out, "My head, my head!" (2 Kings 4:19a, HCSB) A servant was called and carried the child to his mother.

Scripture is brief, to the point: The child sat on her lap until noon and then died. (2 Kings 4:20b, HCSB). The agony of holding and watching what is precious die, must have been an interminable ordeal. It is not hard to imagine her desperation to keep the child from dying. No amount of effort, prayers, or love worked. How often do we see what we had hoped for die before us? How often do we try to change what is happening but it is not in our hands. We are brought to our knees, our hearts are broken. We often rebel, desperate for a miracle to bring what is dying back to life.

Where do we run when beset with such loss? What are we thinking when confronted with disaster? Hearts that are filled with despair turn to things that might make a difference, that might make life well again. The Shunammite woman moves in the one direction she sees hope, to the one possibility where what has happened might be reversed or changed. She runs to the man of God. Forces come upon her to deter her from getting to this holy one of God, but she persists, running and clinging to his feet. We are reminded of the feet of the Holy One of God:

The feet of Jesus, the better part chosen by Mary (Luke 10:41, NKJV)

The feet of Jesus, where Mary fell down, crying out for her dead brother, Lazarus (John 11:32, NKJV)

The feet of Jesus, which Mary anointed with oil and wiped with her hair (John 12:3, NKJV) doing what she could to worship her Lord (Mark 14:8, NKJV)

The feet of Jesus, where the nail of the sin of the world was driven.

The feet of Jesus, where we can pour out our heart's despair and brokenness in loss.

How many times do forces come against our running to Jesus? The way of the world comes against such "foolishness" and we are encouraged to seek deliverance and comfort for the body through medicine, for the mind through counseling and sharing with other humans. How often are we beckoned to come away from clinging to Jesus, clinging to His feet. The Shunammite woman clings to the feet of the man of God and cries out:

"Did I ask my lord for a son? Didn't I say, 'Do not deceive me?'" (2 Kings 4:28, HCSB)

Do not deceive me...is that our cry to the Lord? "Do not deceive me. Spare me the agony of what love costs. Spare me the tragedy of what life often brings. Spare me from the suffering of caring and trying." Is this my cry to the Lord?

But the woman of Shunem is wise in the middle of her crying. She stays right with the man of God. May we stay with Jesus, right with Him and wait upon His power to come, to listen, to abide with us in our anguish. May we stay there long enough for the power of His resurrection love to do its work in our hearts.

Elisha sends his servant, Gehazi, with his staff, a gift from God to lay upon the dead child. It has no effect, no power apart from the man of God. It is only in Elisha's coming, praying, and laying himself upon the child, putting his mouth upon the child's mouth, his eyes upon his eyes, his hands upon his hands, stretching himself upon the child, then only does the flesh of the child wax warm (2 Kings 4:34, KJV). In Elisha, we see God showing us Who He is in loss, our loss, in our suffering.

When the Lord comes to us, He sees things as they are. He sees what is alive, what is dead. He comes upon us in response to our cry, giving Himself to us. How long does He stay upon us where we have died and turned cold? Where our hearts are stilled and dare not flutter to life again because our struggle in life is so costly? He stays upon us until that which is cold and hard, bereft of life, light and warmth becomes softened, warmed in Him. But it is not just flesh warmth, flesh being alive that is needed. It is the spirit that needs to be quickened in us. So it is that the Lord, like Elisha, stretches Himself upon us. He stretches Himself upon our deadness, upon our sin, upon our broken, wounded souls, upon our past until we are completed in becoming alive in Jesus, fully welcoming in His Holy Spirit, getting rid of our own self-spirit completely. Then our eyes open, really open.

For just as the Shunammite's son sneezes and opens his eyes in response to Elisha, Jesus opens our eyes by His holy hand so that we can be taken up, to love and to be loved (verse 36) but not before we have become a people who fall at the Lord's feet (vs. 37) and bow ourselves to the ground before Him.

Lord, enable us to bring our hurting, cold, dead hearts to You, hearts filled up with fear of loss and love failing. Enable us to lie still and be with You as You cover us gently over by Your loving embrace. That as You touch our mouths, our eyes, our hands with Yours:

> We will never speak the same.

> We will never see the same.

> We will never do the same.

Lord, when what is dead and painful in its memory is brought to Your embrace on Your altar for Your will to be done, we are not the same: in the deep heart of the man, of the woman who comes to You, new creation, new life is born anew.

We are redeemed from dust. We are redeemed from dust.

> *My soul, praise the LORD,*
> *and all that is within me, praise His holy name.*

My soul, praise the LORD, and do not forget
    all His benefits.

He forgives all your sin;
He heals all your diseases.
He redeems your life from the pit;
He crowns you with faithful love and compassion.
He satisfies you with goodness; your youth is renewed
    like the eagle.

The LORD executes acts of righteousness
    and justice for all the oppressed.
He revealed His ways to Moses, His deeds to the people
of Israel.
The LORD is compassionate and gracious,
    slow to anger and full of faithful love.
He will not always accuse us or be angry forever.
He has not dealt with us as our sins deserve or repaid us
according to our offenses.

For as high as the heavens are above the earth,
 so great is His faithful love toward those who fear Him.
As far as the east is from the west,
    so far has He removed our transgressions from us.
As a father has compassion on his children,
 so the LORD has compassion on those who fear Him.
For He knows what we are made of, remembering that
    we are dust.
(Psalm 103:1-14, HCSB)

How Long O God?

It is pretty in this open land of fields, streams, and mountains. The day blusters, a fitting metaphor, descriptive of the one You, Lord, have planned for me. He had refused to be seen, but I will no longer prescribe him medicines. Authority over power has won. I believe it is a good ruse for this divine appointment. I am welcomed in. The hearth is warm. Sunlight streams into the chalet.

The lack of food and only sips of liquid do not slow the words of this man. I barely enter the room and introduce myself when the questions begin. "How much longer? Can you do something so I won't suffer?" "I am not afraid of death!" It is the getting there that is the problem.

He is commanding, controls the conversation. I am aware of being jerked along at a pace that is uncomfortable because I do not know him. I learn from him that he is a control freak; he feels many do not understand his lack of fear of death; he is frustrated that every time he goes to sleep and wakes, he has not died yet. He does not want to struggle; he does not want to suffer.

He acknowledges that no one can give an exact time, but certainly an estimate might be possible. How much longer? It is the third time the question has been asked. O Lord, I pray, in desperation for a clue how to reach him. Being a "master" of control has sharpened his skill in hiding and protecting his true heart. I sense this visit is facilitating Your scalpel to find the place where sinew and joint can be divided. The heart of the man would then lie exposed, vulnerable to Your onslaught of love and grace.

He startles me with an abrupt change in tactic. "I know what you are about. The one thing you are after. You don't have to tell me…I know. It is what they," his eyes and small head movements indicate, *the women,* "are after: a deathbed conversion. Not me. I don't believe in it. That's what you want. That's what you are after, isn't it?"

I evade the question: "You are the one who brought it up, Mr. Blair, not I." He has a disdain for those who make deathbed confessions. He is a man who demands justice, tit for tat, you get what you deserve. There is no question, he is prepared to take what he deserves. Besides, he does not believe in heaven or hell anyway. "I am man enough-always have been…to take what I deserve."

Yet, there is a waver in his voice, a shift of his eyes to avoid contact. It sounds like you believe you do not deserve to go to heaven, I say. He describes the kind of man he is, the life he has lived, what he feels he deserves. He definitely "does not deserve to go to heaven."

> *Oh, Mr. Blair, you are absolutely right. You hit the nail on the head. You definitely do not deserve to go to heaven.*

The room fills with silence. My words, clipped, precise, sharp hang in the air. I take his hand…pat it…

> *Neither do I. No one deserves to go to heaven.*
> He recovers. **Oh yes, there are good people. I know some.**
> *No, there is no one who deserves to go to heaven.*
> *The price to be paid is too high, no human can pay it…only Jesus. Only Jesus.*

At Your name, he waves his hand, shakes his head. No…he reiterates his argument about human goodness, though not his. He expresses anger that a supposed God of love could let people suffer in hell. He believes heaven and hell are what you experience here on this earth…in this life.

> *No, I quip. You think you are miserable now? I cannot imagine what kind of misery there is for those who go to hell.*

He gets angry. **You are just saying that to scare me. It won't work.**

Don't worry, sir. You should not get so upset. After all you don't believe in heaven or hell anyway.

Someone chuckles. I realize again that we have an audience. I sense his fatigue. We have talked almost non-stop for 30 minutes. He looks dejected. I pat his hand. This is a lot to think about. What is clear is that you are being pursued, Mr. Blair. You are being pursued by the God who created you. He loves and cares for you that much.

I am glad someone does…the ragged cry ends in a half sob. He quivers. His voice breaks. For a while there, I was so alone…so alone…no one would come around. I had a lot of time to think and wonder what I had done to make people stay away. I have tried to reach out to make amends…but it was…it was really hard. Well, Mr. Blair, I say, "There is a lot to think about."

I ask if I could pray for him. He glances up, almost eager, his eyes beg, his voice feigns nonchalance. I sense his spirit pleading. Your Spirit pours forth the words of Your love, Your desire, Your hope, Your mercy, Your grace. I struggle to keep the sobs from my voice. The tears fall silently; the man before me quivers every now and then. With the Amen, there seems to be a collective sigh.

We exit, the women and I, to the living room. The sunshine filters in. I sit for a minute, still, trying to get my bearings, trying to determine the next steps. Ah yes, prescriptions.

He is in a battle isn't he? The older woman is earnest. We, she indicates her daughter and herself, we are believers. He is in a battle. I look up with a jolt. You are right. You are absolutely right. We speak of the long journey, the pain-filled past two years of unspeakable heartbreak. We have prayed, a lot of people are praying. The acceptance of possible loss is a matter of fact, but hope is palpable, hope is palpable. What weapon is needed O Lord? The only offensive weapon there is…Your WORD. Put on the full armor of

God. Prepare for battle. Finally, be strong in the Lord and in His mighty power.

> Put on the full armor of God so that you can take your stand against the devil's schemes. For our struggle is not against flesh and blood, but against the rulers, against the authorities, against the powers of this dark world, against the spiritual forces of evil in the heavenly realms.
> Stand firm, with the belt of truth buckled around your waist, with the breastplate of righteousness in place, and with your feet fitted with the readiness that comes from the gospel of peace. In addition to all this, take up the shield of faith, with which you can extinguish all the flaming arrows of the evil one. Take the helmet of salvation, and the sword of the Spirit, which is the WORD of God. (Ephesians 6:10-18)

Read him the Word of God. No editorializing…just the WORD of God.

Epilogue, shared by one who loves him:
After you left he asked:

> **Was she a preacher?** *No, she was a doctor.*
> **Was she a plant?** *No, she came because God sent her.*
> **She gave me a lot to think about.**

He slept then and in his sleep, You Lord came and revealed Yourself to him. He awoke and welcomed Your presence, Your love, Your peace. There was a grand celebration with those he loved: family both in blood and spirit who had witnessed so many years to him, who had prayed for him so long: they sang hymns, songs, and praises to You Lord God

And on the 3rd day after he was reborn, he died on the Sabbath day, a day of Jubilee: all the saints clapped their hands as another child of Yours was welcomed home.

The Best Thing

It is a brilliant blue sky day. The house sits on the slant of a hill. Old stones stacked one to another make a wall. The stairs speak of many years and many, many feet. The porch overlooks the valley but I am running late. The view will have to be taken in later. I meet the son, the daughter and the granddaughter. The house is old, filled with character, wooden floors that have long since lost being flat, walls and doors shifted just enough to make you realize the house has settled. I note an oxygen compressor in the living room. In the adjacent front room, with large windows overlooking porch and view, is a hospital bed and, closer to the windows, a recliner chair.

Its occupant looks up. I round the corner of his chair and only too late realize his hands are up ready to take my hand right at the point I first passed him. His granddaughter speaks:

He's blind.
Ah, thank you.

I retrace steps, before I am able to reach his hands.

Where is she?

A strong voice, shock of white hair, eyes dark brown looking intently at me as if he sees me. The handshake is firm and warm.

Good to meet you.
How are you doing?
Not so good. I'm 98…had a little trouble lately.
So they tell me, sir. Looks like you had a fall.

His face is ruggedly handsome. High cheekbones, strong chin; wrinkles are aligned to accommodate the frequent smile. A large bruise on his right temple with dried blood and suture lines speak to his recent battle with weakness and balance.

> *My, you are handsome.*
> **Why, thank you.**

He grins. He is pleased he has been noticed. We talk, his daughter and granddaughter and I. We must get papers signed. His daughter leaves and gets her brother who glances at the papers and signs.

> **Anymore? Papers? To be signed? That's it?**
> *Yes, that's it.*
> **Okay.**

He exits to the porch while his father sleeps off and on. His daughter and granddaughter share his story of increasing weight loss, fragility and weakness, of episodes of confusion and one episode recently of unresponsiveness.

They are torn about hospice care, comfort care and their desire to treat what can be treated if it is simple. The struggle to do something to maintain and preserve life as long as possible, but not to such aggressive intervention, is a challenge between heart and mind. The mind sees the decline, acknowledges the age, and understands the futility of aggressive intervention. The heart remembers the good times, the routine of an active life, and hopes for the possibilities of a continued life lived well. Reality must tie the two together. It is not an easy task. Usually the heart loses. The hope must be reframed from cure and health to living well as best one can with what one has until that final call home.

We turn to him who has been the object of conversation. He sleeps, undisturbed in his rugged handsomeness. He easily rouses and accommodates with equanimity being fussed over, wounds undressed, cleansed and redressed. He is quite drowsy. At my offer to say a blessing for him he looks up, eyes curiously now focused, bright, inquisitive.

**Prayer? …Now that's the best thing I've heard
all day. Yup, am 98 years old. Go to church
three times a week. Prayer…that's mighty fine.**

We sit before You, the birds sing, the oxygen hums. We give
thanks. We worship. We praise You the author of life and blessing.
We give thanks for You indeed are good. Your love endures forever.
We pray for Your wisdom, Your healing hand according to Your
will and Your timing. We pray for time to celebrate his life and
Your love and for him to enjoy the love present in this home. We
pray and say Amen.

That is the best thing you've done all morning.

We laugh and praise Your Name.

Longing for God

Parched lips, gaunt, long bones, skin so tight every movement creates pain. The cancer eats at lung and bone; to breathe, to move is to hurt. Please, he cries, I hurt. Please, outstretched hands grope across bare mattress. His words are brief. There is no energy to say much, just signing papers and getting checked tax an already exhausted spirit, mind and body.

> *...sighing comes to me instead of food;*
> *my groans pour out like water*
> *What I have feared has come upon me;*
> *what I dreaded has happened to me.*
> *I have no peace, no quietness; I have no rest, but only*
> *turmoil.*
>
> *Now my life ebbs away; days of suffering grip me.*
> *Night pierces my bones. My gnawing pains never rest,*
> *the churning inside me never stops.*
> *Days of suffering confront me.*
> *...my skin grows black and peels. My body burns with fever*
> *My harp is tuned to mourning and my flute to the sound of wailing.*
> *(adapted from Job 3:24-26; 30:16-17, 30-31 NIV)*
>
> *Mercy, O Lord, mercy. We cry out for mercy.*
> *Hear our cry O Lord... Hear our cry.*

It is hard to know what to say. Plans for a hospital bed, pressure mattress, pain medication prompt a cry and sobs. "You believe me!" A shudder goes through the bent frame, a sigh escapes, death's grip slips. Your light enters his darkness. His startled cry pierces the quiet: "I am really hurting." He sobs. He reaches in thankfulness, he gropes on the bare mattress pulling forward, his eyes wild, his lips so parched, a grimace between pain and hope.

How much he suffers, O Lord. How much he suffers
My God, my God have mercy. Please have mercy.
You are our refuge and strength, an ever present help in trouble.
Therefore we will not fear, though the earth give way,
the mountains fall into the heart of the sea,
though its waters roar and foam
    and the mountains quake with their surging.
There is a river whose streams make glad the city of God,
the Holy Place where the Most High dwells...
Be still. Be still and know that I am God.
I will be exalted among the nations.
    I will be exalted on the earth.
(adapted from Psalm 46, NIV)

I offer to say a prayer for him. He looks up startled. His eyes for the first time have a glimmer of life. "Yes," he mouths, his skeleton hands grope desperately, outstretched, offering his suffering: "Yes, please."

Speak Your Word my Lord. Speak Your Word.

Come to Me, all you who are weary and heavy burdened,
    of Me,
for I am gentle and humble in heart.
    You will find rest for your souls,
For My yoke is easy, My burden light.
(adapted from Matthew 11:28-30, RSV)

Praise be to the God and Father of our Lord Jesus Christ.
The Father of compassion, the God of all comfort,
Who comforts us in all our troubles
    so that we can comfort
those in any trouble with the comfort we ourselves have
received from God.
For just as the sufferings of Christ flow over
    into our lives,
so also through Christ our comfort overflows.
(adapted from 2 Corinthians 1:3-5, NIV)

Nothing Shall Separate Us

She met me at the door: her face haggard, worn. Her shoulders weighted down, her eyes swollen. The shadows and weariness of her skin about her eyes made me stop in my tracks. My bag, though heavy, stayed still at my side. We were poised for bad news. It had been a horrible week, just horrible. In what way horrible? I asked softly. I imagined him taking a sudden turn for the worse: short of breath, chest pain, pneumonia. But it was an accident, one that left him with great loss of dignity and left her with a mess all over him, all over his clothes, all over the carpet. It was the carpet that was the worst. She could not take it up and discard it because it was soiled. All the other clothing touched by the earthiest part of a human's life was easily tossed.

I set my bag down at this and searched the woman's face. She was utterly worn out. This was near breakpoint. It is for many, something about incontinence and helplessness that undo the resolve to keep on keeping on. It is too graphic a reminder of loss, a signal of worse to come. Her face contorted in pain; her voice barely above a whisper.

I can't take much more…I can't take much more. I don't think he can stay here.

The repetition sounded an alarm in me, one which clamored loudly in my heart. This was going to be very hard. The two of them were very close. He was utterly spoiled by her devotion, her attention to providing him three well thought out meals a day, a house ordered, clean and neat and always elegantly presentable. He was a man of leisure and had been for some time. She had taken pride in keeping him so, spoiling him and loving him by her deeds and quick response to everything he asked. His medication was impeccably ordered. The medication adjustments made, fine-tuned amazingly correct by her attention to detail, the smallest evidence of edema in his legs or increased shortness of breath clued her to increase the fluid pill or to call me. There was no worry about his medical care. She was one of the best and he knew it. She had adjusted to tending to pressure sores, to small incontinent accidents, to lack of getting out, to the endless cycle of washing, cooking, cleaning, to just being contained in the four walls with TV and husband, his illness and occasional visits from children, her entire world.

But recently, she had been sick with the flu, bedridden for almost five days. It had left her exhausted and vulnerable. He could not remember the accident. All was the same to him except he was only "fair." He rarely complained; he usually painted things better than they were.

The familiar joking between the two of them is peculiarly missing. Its absence grips me, even the cat wants out. It does not linger or lounge on the bed as is its custom. I have had many talks that stretch me, but this, this conversation will be very hard. He is not fully aware of what is going on and at this time in his life, change will be traumatic.

I search his face, it is filled with something different from sadness; the worry lines between his eyes speak of fear. He is not as unaware as I had thought.

> *What is your biggest concern?*
> **My wife.**
> *In what way?*
> **She's having to work her butt off for me.**
> *And what is your worry about that?*
> **She will get worn out and ...** his voice trails

off.

> *It is a dilemma, isn't it?*

Yes.

We talk then about his increasing weakness, the frailty of his heart, the faltering of his breathing, the failing of his memory, the fatigue that confines him from bed to chair and requires two to assist him to move.

What choices, what possibilities might there be?
Need help…need to get her help. I don't want to go to a nursing home. And she would never think to put me in one.

His words hang in the air. I do not know what to say. The silence fills the room. She sits quietly on the far side of the bed; her silence speaks volumes. He adds hesitantly:

I don't think she would.

He stops. I recognize his well-worn pattern of speech: first, a hesitant statement then a query to his wife for confirmation. The need for confirmation and affirmation had become more frequent as of late.

Would you? …Honey?

It was both statement and question. She is drawn into herself. She hesitates, clears her throat and begins to speak about her friends who have their husbands in nursing homes, they like it, it works well, her words tumble over each other.

Well, I wouldn't want to go.

We sit still then, very still.

Well.

I start but am not really sure what to say; my inside voice is clamoring: *Lord, Lord.*

His wife moved then to check his medicines; it is time for his pill. She swiftly picks the right one out and gives it to him. He takes it obediently at her words.

It would be really hard, really hard, she says.

She describes his day in their home: chair to bed to bathroom, what he likes, how confined he is, how they cannot get a wheelchair in and out of the room, how much more he would be able to get out of these four walls. Her emphasis on the four walls resonates.

I am staring blankly out of the window. My heart hears Your soft words Lord.

**Love Me, love Me with all your heart, mind
and soul and love each other as I have loved
you. Love each other as I have loved you.**

If one loves You, Lord with all one's being, it would be to You an act of worship, of thanksgiving for all the blessing You have poured out and are pouring out. In worship, joy abounds and in joy abounding, the heart overflows to willingly sacrifice for the other.

What is your main priority? I gently ask.
The children.

*Yes, they are living their own lives pretty much right
now?*
He nods.

*Right now, right here, in your home what is your
main priority?*

He looks blankly at me.

*It is to love the Lord with all your heart, with all
your mind, with all your strength, with all your
soul.*

His face shifts, his eyes light up.

Yes, of course.
And as a man of God, your next priority has always been to provide for your wife and your children?

He nods.

As the man of this home and a man who loves the Lord, what would you still want to do?
Take care of my wife.
Yes, even as you are right now.

My heart fills up. I hear her quiet sobs, then sounds of sniffing and shifting. He looks up and stares.

She left the room, he whispers, **she is crying.**

We sit then. Somewhere in the conversation he had reached for my hand. I cannot speak. It is too much. The tears begin to over flow their boundaries, cascading down, dropping onto my shirt. I sit very still trying to get a grip: Lord, Lord, please help.

A tissue is awkwardly shoved into my face catching tears. I almost laugh, it is a good gift of grace.

Thank you.
I will be all right.

I nod, we talk then of options, his wife re-enters the room. There are many options, many possibilities.

You must call the children and talk.

He is silent but his shoulders are up.

You are in a battle, the hardest last game, sir. You must play it well, the way you would want as a man who loves God and desires to take care of those you love. You are in a battle and you must be well-armed. You must read His Word every day. You must meet with Jesus every day. What you believe about God must be more than words in your mouth. It

*must become the armor in which you go into playing
this hardest game, this biggest battle. You must pray
a lot.*

He nods, his eyes steadfast, and blue. His resolve is settled:

We will call the children and talk.

Let's pray then.

He grips my hand tighter. It is a hard prayer; You undo us
Lord with Your grace, with Your mercy to us in our ordinary lives.
We do not deserve such generosity. You provide. You guide. You
are present. You are love. Without You we are nothing, without
You we cannot get beyond ourselves. Without You, our suffering
has no meaning and nothing eternally good can come out of pain
or sorrow. But we, in You, are more than conquerors in all things:

Who shall separate us from the love of Christ? Shall
trouble or hardship or persecution or famine or nakedness or danger or sword? As it is written:
"For Your sake we face death all day long; we are
considered as sheep to be slaughtered." (adapted
from Romans 8:35-36, NIV)

Death has its way with all humans, but in all these things we
are more than conquerors through You Lord Jesus who loves us.

Nothing can separate us from You, nothing created,
neither death nor life, neither angels nor demons,
neither the present nor the future, nor any powers,
neither height nor depth, nor anything else in all creation will be able to separate us from Your love O,
God that is in Christ Jesus our Lord. (adapted from
Romans 8:37-39, NIV)

Faithful Creator

**It is like having four children and one of them
is missing.**
**I know I only have three children, but one of
them is gone.**
It is that deep of a sadness?
Yes.

He whispers and his eyes so blue, brim full. We are sitting in
a starkly concrete room, two hospital beds, linoleum floors, partly
drawn brown curtain, plain brown chest of drawers, so worn and
old, white institutional sheets, geri-chair, plastic hospital mattress,
and bedside table. It is as much a nursing home as one can get,
even the view to an empty courtyard filled with sparse grass and
the other side of the u-shaped building.

What a change, what a loss from his previous home. We sit
very still, his left hand in mine. His sadness fills me and we are very
quiet. The neighbor's TV blares.

Are you angry?
No…he says simply.
Are you hurt? A little hesitation.
No, mostly sad, mostly sad.
Yes, I can see that.
She needed help.
Yes, she did.
**I would do anything that would be best for her
with my situation.**
*You are saying you are willing to make what sacri-
fice you need to take care of her?*

He looks up, gazes hard at me…his eyes fill up. He nods.

But it is hard…very hard.

He nods again. He is a man who does not speak his emotions very often. His eyes betray a depth of feeling that at times is unreadable and yet perhaps words would not speak to the sadness and grief deep within. He has never been one to complain. When bad things happen, he picks up, shrugs it off and carries on. This is one of the hardest things though, one of the hardest: not being surrounded by people familiar to him who dote on him. Here, he is one of many.

> *You have become weaker?*
> **Yes.**
> *Where does God fit in, in all of this?*
> **At the top…at the top.**
> *Meaning?*
> **In it all…** he whispers.
> *If you did not have the Lord, this would be unbearable?*

His lip trembles at that. He squeezes tight on my hand. My tears held in check drop onto the white institutional sheet. We sit in silence a long time.

> *There is a passage, you might remember of John the Baptist telling his disciples that he must become less as Jesus becomes more?*

He nods.

> *All this.*

I motion with my hand to his surroundings.

> *and what your body is doing is very hard.*
> *Becoming less is always very hard.*

He searches my face.

And it is then that Jesus can become stronger in us.

He sighs, leans back on the pillow nodding yes. We sit a long time, quiet. He speaks then about his children, about missing them. I observe how reserved he is in his suffering.

Always been that way.
God knows your suffering. He is okay with your tears. It is part of becoming less and sacrificing for others. You are doing what He asks, loving Him with all your heart and loving others just as you are loved.

His head picks up at that, he nods, his blue eyes look at me, back and forth across my face.

That is worship... He nods.
Do you read the Bible?
My neighbor reads it to me.
That is a blessing.
Yes.
Do you pray?
All the time.
That is good. Why don't we do that now.
Yes...and he gathers my small hand in his big one.

At the Amen, his eyes again search my face and then he begins to cry. It is a deep weeping that wants so desperately to come out. He allows it voice for only a few minutes. He looks away, composes himself and looks back at me. His lip trembles, his eyes brim again. His breathing strains hard. His pulse palpable through his hand which is holding mine quickens. We sit a long time waiting while his heart catches up with the hard work of crying. Even that momentary release was at a cost.

Suffering in You, Lord, has redemption. Suffering without You is great darkness. We are grateful for the comfort You are, Lord.

You are our only Comfort in life, our only true Comfort in life. Give him Your peace. Fill him up with Your fullness. Help him know Your love that surpasses knowledge. Help him know, for his blessing and for Your glory. Amen and Amen.

> Blessed be the God and Father of our Lord Jesus Christ, who according to His abundant mercy has begotten us again to a living hope through the resurrection of Jesus Christ from the dead, to an inheritance incorruptible and undefiled and that does not fade away, reserved in heaven for you, who are kept by the power of God through faith for salvation ready to be revealed in the last time.
>
> In this you greatly rejoice, though now for a little while, if need be, you have been grieved by various trials, that the genuineness of your faith, being much more precious than gold that perishes, though it is tested by fire, may be found to praise, honor, and glory at the revelation of Jesus Christ, whom having not seen you love. Though now you do not see Him, yet believing, you rejoice with joy inexpressible and full of glory, receiving the end of your faith—the salvation of your souls...
>
> But when you do good and suffer, if you take it patiently, this is commendable before God. For to this you were called, because Christ also suffered for us, leaving us an example, that you should follow His steps:
>
> "Who committed no sin, nor was deceit found in His mouth"; who when He was reviled, did not revile in return; when He suffered, He did not threaten, but committed Himself to Him who judges righteously; who Himself bore our sins in His own body on the tree, that we, having died to sins, might live for righteousness—by whose stripes you were healed. For you were like sheep going astray, but have now returned to the Shepherd and Overseer of your souls...

Beloved, do not think it strange concerning the fiery trial which is to try you as though some strange thing happened to you; but rejoice to the extent that you partake of Christ's sufferings, that when His glory is revealed, you may also be glad with exceeding joy. Yet if anyone suffers as a Christian, let him not be ashamed, but let him glorify God in this matter... Therefore let those who suffer according to the will of God commit their souls to Him in doing good, as to a faithful Creator. (adapted from 1 Peter 1:3-9; 2:20-25; 4:12-13, 16,19, NKJV)

In Your Presence is Fullness of Joy

In Your Presence is Fullness of Joy
At Your right hand are pleasures forever more.
(Psalm 16:11, NKJV)

There is one thing, one thing that I seek, that I may behold Your beauty and to inquire at Your temple. You say to seek You Lord, to be in Your presence, to seek Your beauty, to inquire at Your temple, for this is one's spiritual act of worship. How does one "be" in Your presence? How does one seek Your beauty? How does one inquire at Your temple?

By worship and the Word. Your Word breathed into life. Your Word spoken before time began. Your Word made flesh and dwelt among us.

There on one seat after another…a total of four to be exact are the same Bibles, not the standard KJV that graces most of the laps and seats of those at the service, not a NKJV either. It is a new one that seems unfamiliar. Different. You can sense it from the cover but because it has Bible in its title, one surmises that Your Word is in it and Your Word become flesh is its focus. Whose are those? Why did someone pick that one out? Why four copies?

You can find out if you go next door and see him who is drinking coffee.

He, who is drinking coffee is also the one who plays bass, is also the one who drives teens around listening to idle chatter and tries in a fatherly way to steer the conversation to one that edifies You, Lord. He exhorts the participants to a higher call than the ordinary world-life that woos young adults to stay dead to real life, living lives which make it but not to living life abundantly.

Next door is a continuous "coffee shop" of the most ordinary kind. The double arches, bright in their neon yellow are familiar and more welcome than the red, white and blue, visible in many areas of the world where people hunger and starve not only for bread but for the very bread of life that enables life abundant. In walking by once, noting what is absorbing the attention of the one who chose the "different" Bibles, I pray for wisdom about interrupting the reverie of one who appears to be taking a break. But Lord, You know, there is a soul out there hungering for Your Word that is more easily understood than the KJV that I read to her last week. She looked at me uncomprehendingly, and when I read from the NLB; she stopped and marveled that it was the same Scripture. Little did he know that it was her tears, her yearning to know and understand the Word more that prompted the interruption of the coffee break at the Double Arches Café.

Why? And what is it that makes it different? And how did you arrive at that particular one? And how do you like it? And what does your wife and children think? And many more questions. Is it true to the central message of the Lord's Word? Are there areas you don't particularly agree with? The patience in which the questions were thoughtfully considered and then carefully answered spoke to the seriousness of the issue, the time it took to come to a prayerful decision. It gave a glimpse of a different side of a man who in worship practice revels in dry humor, jokes that take a moment to gather in and enjoy and whose insight into people's nature triggers a mirthful outlook, a willingness to give and take, and a patience that probably gets tripped into poking fun to cajole another to try something different.

> **It speaks the Truth and when things in the
> King James are confusing or unclear, the
> meaning behind and in the words is revealed in**

**the translation. It has been one that is good for
the whole family.**

His words are echoed by his wife. She is quiet, gentle, insight-
ful. Her sensitive spirit has picked up on newcomers alone, unsure.
She has spoken words of welcome and prayed for them enabling
them to have a sense of belonging even though who they are is not
yet known. She surprised me when she confided that she did not
know many in the church, alluding to her quiet, somewhat shy way.
That had not been apparent when the Holy Spirit had moved her
to welcome me to be a part of the church family. It is good, Lord,
that You so often confirm Your will in answer to prayer, through
Your Word and through the ordinary circumstances of our lives.
This translation will be a good fit for the one You have given a
hunger for Your Word.

You keep it in the box?
**Yes, it is that special to me. I take it out every
day when I read it and when I am through I
put it back in. You have no idea what this Bible
means to me, how it speaks to me.**

Her last words are barely audible. She, such a gentle spirit,
trembles and carefully lifts the Bible out. Her fingers linger on the
cover as she hands it to me. The tears, so close, waver in her eyes.
How she loves You, Lord, a sweet, simple, joyous love.

Shall I read?
Yes, yes...I was hoping you would.

It has been a usual home medical visit. Adjusting of medication, listening to concerns and fine tuning care. Yet, it always
comes down to the deepest hunger of this woman: a hunger for
Your Word, O Lord, and for You. You feed her Your Word of Life.
Your Word made flesh gathers with us as Your Word is sent out.
You accomplish Your purpose through it, Lord. And she, contrite
in heart and spirit, trembles at Your Word.

The LORD is my light and my salvation—
    whom should I fear?
The LORD is the stronghold of my life—
    of whom should I be afraid?

When evildoers came against me to devour my flesh,
my foes and my enemies stumbled and fell.

Though an army deploy against me,
my heart is not afraid;
though war break out against me,
still I am confident.

I have asked one thing from the LORD;
it is what I desire:
to dwell in the house of the LORD
all the days of my life,
gazing on the beauty of the LORD AND seeking [Him] in
His temple.

For He will conceal me in His shelter
in the day of adversity;
He will hide me under the cover of His tent;
He will set me high on a rock.

Then my head will be high
above my enemies around me;
I will offer sacrifices in His tent with shouts of joy.
I will sing and make music to the LORD.

LORD, hear my voice when I call;
be gracious to me and answer me.

In Your behalf my heart says, "Seek My face."
LORD, I will seek Your face.

Do not hide Your face from me;
do not turn Your servant away in anger.

You have been my help;
do not leave me or abandon me,
God of my salvation.

Even if my father and mother abandon me,
the LORD cares for me.

Because of my adversaries,
show me Your way, LORD,
and lead me on a level path.

Do not give me over to the will of my foes,
for false witnesses rise up against me,
breathing violence.

I am certain that I will see the LORD's goodness
in the land of the living.

Wait for the LORD;
be courageous and let your heart be strong.
Wait for the LORD. (adapted from Psalms 27, HCSB)

She has waited a long time Lord for Your written Word to be available in large enough print for her waning eyes and straightforwardly translated without losing its beauty or meaning. Such is the work of Your Holy hands, of Your Holy planning, of putting four Bibles in a row, and Your Holy Spirit moving to obedience, the hearts of Your children.

In Your Presence is Fullness of Joy
At Your right hand are pleasures forever more.
(Psalms 16:11, NKJV)

Longing for Your Judgment

He is a big, burly man: big and tall, rough, rugged, tough. He holds his left hand firmly over an object. There is blood and grime caked on his hand, running over his knuckles, his fingers, the crevices of his fingernails. He fidgets and sighs every now and then.

> *What d'ye do?*
> **Trying to take a huge bass off my lure. It was thrashing and first thing I know, my lure is in my hand.**
> *Oh. What happened to the fish?*
> **It got away.**

The sigh, the depth of disappointment, is sharp and deep, filling him up.

> **I shoulda just stayed…shoulda just taped it up and stayed…was in competition and we was doing great until this.**

He looks up gazing past me, his eyes lit with the fire of a man in love… with fishing.

> **They was biting fierce and we were hooking 'em. I shoulda stayed.**
> *Well, it probably was wise you did not. Sure have bled with it.*
> **Yea, tried to get my buddy to hep me. He got sorta sickish. Told him to step on my hand while I tried to yank it out. He got sick, told**

me to go to the doctor. He's a wimp. Shoulda
stayed, not listened to him. Shoulda stayed.
Well, you can't just yank it out you know. It's got a
barb on the other side of the hook. It won't come out
without being cut out.
Oh.

He seems to return to the task at hand. Let me think I say…
usually we have to cut the hook and push it forward and out, does
less tissue damage…His audible sucked in breath stops me.

Yes?
Uh, that is a rare lure, can't buy 'em anymore.

For the first time I notice the "lure." It is a small fish about
the size of one of my fingers. It shimmers in the fluorescent lights.
The rainbow colors on its silver, pale green sides, reminds me of
rainbow trout.

Is it a baby rainbow?
Naw, just a lure, fish like'em.
Hmmm, sure is pretty.
Yea…he says with affection.

The hook is short, attached to two others at the mouth of the
small fish. At its tail is another set of triplet hooks. The barbs, the
hooks are sharp. I move the hook to look at it better. His breath
sucks sharply in again.

Sorry, the angle is odd. Think if I cut it to push it forward it
may make it worse. It'll go into the palm of your hand and that…
that would be bad. Let me think about it. (Translation: let me pray
about it.)

We set up then; his eyes grow wide when he sees all the equip-
ment. He cringes as I tape up the two exposed hooks adjacent to
the one in his hand…for protection against further injury. He is
especially alert when I ask for an 11 blade. He looks over at his wife
when he sees the length and size of the needle.

*Don't worry, that one doesn't go in you, just drawing
up your numbing medicine.*

Before I can anesthetize, numb it up, it must first be cleansed, cleansed with antiseptic. Gloved up, peering closely at the hook in the hand, I make the first attempt at cleansing. The hook moves readily. His muscles flinch but the man does not say a thing. Little if any grime is visibly removed in the first washing. With lots of antiseptic and more awareness of the pain of the man, You commend me to take deep care in washing, in washing the man's hand. I take a deep breath and pray silently, settling my heart into Your patience, Your timing, Your care, Your way of seeing.

We are all wounded creatures, O Lord. Often self-inflicted but many times our wounds come to us without our acquiesced participation. So often the external dirt and grime mixed with the loss of something alive in us cakes the wound, covers it up, making it fester and grow worse in darkness, deep inside. The wound remains and eats away at our souls. Often we clean up on the outside making ourselves and it, the wound, presentable to the world. We go about with wounded spirits, part of us dying due to the lack of true healing. At times, the inner un-wellness rises up to torment the soul and we respond to another circumstance or person in a way that reflects the deep root of pain we are carrying. And the festering deepens. A little leaven works through the whole. Where, O where is healing? Is there no balm in Gilead? You Lord, who are holy, righteous and just, stand in judgment over all who live. You see all. You see our dying, our festering, our suffering. And we stand aloof from Your presence, spurning Your cleansing by the washing of Your Word, afraid of more pain, afraid of being exposed in truth, afraid of being healed, and being called out of where we have become comfortable. You, Lord, cry out:

*You will be ever hearing but never understanding,
You will be ever seeing but never perceiving.
For this people's heart has become calloused;
They hardly hear with their ears and they have closed*

their eyes,
Otherwise they might see with their eyes, hear with
their ears,
Understand with their hearts and turn, and I would heal
them.
 (adapted from Matthew 13:14-15, NIV)

And in Jeremiah:

...I will restore you to health and heal your wounds...
because you are called an outcast... for whom no one
cares. (adapted from Jeremiah 30:17, NIV)

How do we respond? Will we turn to You, present-
ing ourselves to Your judgment to be delivered from
that which bears so heavily in and upon us? You who
have born all the pain and suffering of our souls and
paid the price for our wounds, have set us free. Will
we turn to You and be freed? Does our soul break
with longing for Your judgments O Lord at all times?
(adapted from Psalm 119:20)

Come let us return to the Lord.
He has torn us to pieces but He will heal us;
He has injured us but He will bind up our wounds.
After two days He will revive us; on the third day
He will restore us that we may live in His presence.
(adapted from Hosea 6:1-2, NIV)

It is the slow, deliberate cleansing of wounds, cleaning periph-
erally first then more centrally at the exact point of pain that makes
me aware of what an act of love this slow washing is. The gentle
laying down of antiseptic soaked gauze, light touch, repetitive,
over and over, that begins to lift the caked on grime. The wound
begins to be exposed in its nakedness. It is time to anesthetize and
cut out that which fills the wound. The first injection before the
numbing takes effect is always hardest. It is best to go into the
already cut wound. The nerve endings have already been severed,

the pain intense but not as intense as if one injects into nearby uninjured normal skin. Do You do that, Lord? Aim Your cleansing sword directly into the wound? No beating about the bush, quick, decisive? Do we flinch and draw away? Can we stay at the point of pain long enough for You to do Your work?

He is grateful for the numbing and looks intently with me at the hook in his hand. It looks different now, visible hook and small bit of flesh surrounded by sterile blue towels. It seems as if it is a separate part of the man. The hook can be moved; it does not go forward or back, only side to side. The flesh is not so willing to give up its barb. The sharp 11 blade scalpel is unsheathed. The man looks on. I do not give him time to protest, just at the point of the hook, a quick incision is made. The barb moves under steady pressure being backed out almost against its will. The flesh clings and must be cut from the hook. It comes free and lure and hook are dropped below the blue towels. Blood gushes from the fresh incision: a cleansing flow washing, washing, washing the wound clean. It eases slowly to a trickle, then to an ooze, then it stops. The wound is tiny, closed, the swelling and outrage of the flesh against the barb is gone. Were it not for the tiny line on the hand, one would think it normal.

> **Looks good?**
> *Yes, but inside it is damaged, needs time to heal, could possibly get infected. It is not well yet. You will need to cleanse it well every day and keep the antibiotic ointment on it. Call us at the first sign of infection. Call us at the first sign of something going wrong. Call us.*

Call on Me, You say, O Lord. Call on Me:

*I cry aloud to the Lord
I lift up my voice to the Lord for mercy.
I pour out my complaint before Him; before Him, I tell my trouble.
When my spirit grows faint within me,*

it is You who watch over my way...
I cry to You, O Lord;
I say, "You are my refuge, my portion
        in the land of the living."
Listen to my cry for I am in desperate need,
rescue me from those who pursue me
for they are too strong for me.
Set me free from my prison, that I may praise Your
name. (adapted from Psalm 142:1-3, 5-7, NIV)

Let the morning bring me word of Your unfailing love,
For I have put my trust in You.
Show me the way to go, for to You I lift up my soul.
Rescue me from my enemies, O Lord,
        for I hide myself in You.
Teach me to do Your will for You are my God.
You are my God. (adapted from Psalm 143:8-10, NIV)

Seeing

She stares out of the window, head turned, intensely concentrating, furrowed brow and deep sadness welling in her eyes.

When you are not needed, they don't want you.
When you are not needed…they don't want
you.

The words slow, halt, burn, eat away the sunlight that filters into the neat, orderly room. The pictures of family, grandchildren, children, the cards, the lift chair in the corner, a gift, contradict her words.

I only ask for a visit once or twice a week.
That is all.
Just to see them once or twice.

Her voice trails. We sit, silently. The pain of loneliness, isolation begs for relief. We talk of her loss of vision, inability to see the TV, inability to read even large print and her early bedtime of 6:30 pm.

What else is there to do?

We talk of her fears of the upcoming winter, the threat of the loss of electricity and loss of oxygen. We ponder her inability to turn the reserve tank of oxygen on and when she should get a replacement and how she would know that.

We sit side by side, her left hand resting near me. As I check her, her hand rests on my knee. I realize how touch must be soothing and scarce. Touch from You, O Lord, would be so wonderful. Your Word is that touch. She cannot read Your word. Her eyes are unable. I wonder aloud if she remembers Scripture. She declares she knows none. She muses about my coming and about going to a nursing home, worried about losing me if she does. She smiles then, a memory stirs and she shares about a recent visit from her son.

I told him the most important reason I want you to come is because you have prayer with me. I feel so much better after you leave. He took my breath away then. He took my breath away. He asked me if I would like to pray with him then, and he said a prayer. It was good. A faint smile creases her lined face. He's got to clean up his language some, but it was good.

She asks me about a dog, she believes it is outside her window, about shadows that move that look like people. There is a tension in the air when she queries the space around her wondering what her eyes are telling her. Her fear is palpable. I wonder out loud if she might know a Psalm that she could say when she is afraid. The only one is Psalm 23. I start slowly:

The LORD is my shepherd...

In unison she haltingly joins in:

I shall not want.
He maketh me lie down in green pastures,

She stumbles over the words, stopping mid-sentence then picking up again.

He leadeth me beside the still waters. He re-
stores my soul.

Her voice strengthens a tad.

He leadeth me in the paths of righteousness,
for His name's sake.

She echoes for His Name's sake, her head lifts up. She sees past my bent frame kneeling beside her.

Yea, though I walk through the valley of the
shadow of death, I shall fear no evil.

Her voice now stronger is firm.

**For Thou art with me. Thy rod and thy staff
they comfort me.**

She stops and does not pick up.

*Thou preparest a table before me in the presence of
mine enemies.*

I stumble over the exact wording from the King James.

Thou anointest my head with oil...

She begins to nod.

My cup runneth over...

She joins me.

My cup runneth over.

Then together, slowly, deliberately:

**Surely goodness and mercy shall follow me all
the days of my life,
And I will dwell in the house of the Lord forever.**

She repeats:

**And I will dwell in the house of the Lord for-
ever.**

We pray. She takes my hands into hers, rests them on her
knees. I kneel before her, her couch the altar on which she sits
before You, Lord. I pray for Your peace, Lord. We recount Your
words and they comfort:

Rejoice in the Lord always. I say it again: Rejoice!
Let your gentleness be evident to all. The Lord is near.
Do not be anxious about anything,
    but in everything,

By prayer and petition with thanksgiving, present
your requests to God.
And the peace of God, which transcends all understanding,
Will guard your hearts and your minds in Christ Jesus. (Philippians 4:4-7, NIV)

She thanks me for taking time to be with a crazy woman. I
thank her for the blessing of being with her and being crazy together. We laugh, she becomes animated, light shines from her eyes.

**You have done a work O God of light…You
have done a work.**

The phone rings. I pat her hand and rise to leave as she talks.
I almost reach the door when she cries out and motions with her
hand. The phone lies discarded on the sofa. She struggles to her
feet. I return swiftly to check her only to catch her words:

You cannot leave without a hug.

I am caught in a warm hug and soft kiss to my cheek. She
squeezes me one last time and as I turn to pull the door close, she
settles. There is peace, Your peace, Lord, and Your light.

All Good Things Must Come to an End

All good things must come to an end...

He is so solemn as he speaks, his face puffy from a process deep within his body that neither he nor I can do anything about. His eyes, deep in thought stare fully at me. He is tall, very tall, and his entire frame seems taller and thinner in the large chair. His face flickers momentarily with a twinge of pain, a heart pain not cardiac but of the soul:

> **My granddaughter,** he whispers, **she will miss her pawpaw. She calls me every night.**

We sit a long time. it is very quiet. It is one of many times of quiet, hand in hand, sitting, allowing Your presence to bathe us in Your peace, Your comfort which we need so desperately. It has been a rough year: postural hypotension, blood pressure dropping with an upright positioning kept him from getting up and about. It was a product of a strange Parkinson-like illness that was not Parkinson's but was a good wanna-be look alike that even the medicines to treat Parkinson's seemed to help. It took a wonderfully gifted neurologist to find the right amount of medicine, far exceeding the usual prescribed dose, that finally brought this man three or four months of getting stronger, getting about more independently, allowing a sense of well-being and hope for continued enjoyment in this life on earth. Then came the abdominal pain that jolted all of us awake to the temporariness of the frailty of human bodies. It let us know that something deeper was going on. It was an unusual kind of illness, a cancer whose tissue type was not readily amenable to being deciphered to give guidance to care and treatment. Eventually, it was determined by actual surgery that it had spread already. It was best to leave things as is and wait. How different Your seeing and knowing is than ours. You've known all along because You know the whole, You know the end from the beginning. We see so dimly, Lord and when we do see, we do not interpret correctly much of the time.

There followed a season of "getting better," of uneventful days of "doing fine." A routine of care around taking medication, tube feedings, physical therapy, swallowing exercises and treatment and contented sitting in living room listening to music or sermons. At times the contentedness was interrupted with an anxious desire to do more, to not be so dependent, to be stronger. But many times, there was a settling in of the soul in realization that You, O Lord, had his life in Your hand. His wife of many years was meticulous in his care, always hoping, always trying, always serving, always wanting to give and give more and love and love more. And the son, silent yet strongly present, would intermittently come in to ask questions during the visits. His matter-of-fact take care attitude was a solid comfort to the father. He gave his parents such an abiding deep respect and honor in his take-care attitude that the trust and certainty that what needed to be done would be done well, efficiently and on time. It seems that the son is the apple that has not fallen far from the tree, for the father's deepest desire throughout all his illness was to take care of his family. Such deep care had become part of the legacy from father to son.

We spent much time talking about how he used to do that, care for his family, through his work, bringing home the bacon the old-fashioned way. We spent more time wondering how he would do that emotionally, spiritually sharing his deep abiding love to this precious family about him. There were days of sharing about God's call on him to be spiritual head of house, leading his family to love and reverence You, O Lord, King of kings and Lord of lords, and to be in relationship with You, the Living God through the best of times and the worst of times.

These sessions stretched us both. He in his quiet reserved man ways where deep heart issues are so privately kept, challenged me to utterly depend upon You, Lord in how to speak, when to be silent, how to ask the questions that would open up the heart rather than close it to more open expressions of love. His quietly deep, utterly respectable repose would occasionally be undone by a wave of emotion: tears trembling in voice and spirit, we would be touched by Your grace, his ever thankful spirit giving voice to all the blessing he could see even in the middle of his suffering.

The hardest part was the realization that he was not going to get better. In two weeks, the growing weakness, the increasing shortness of breath, the gain of weight and abdominal girth that spoke un-wellness, not healthy gain, brought us all that day of hard questions.

When will I get better, doc?

Long silence. I am unable to ask him his opinion right after he asked me such a question. His characteristically sparse use of words make it seem disrespectful to not answer his question directly. Long breath in, deep prayer, Lord help, quieted my soul.

> *Your physical body is very frail, sir. It is unable to*
> *fight the battle anymore. This is bigger than you or I.*
> **How long?**

I do not know, but am unable to speak any words. His face queries me further. I feel compelled to not evade.

> *It would be a wonderful blessing if the Lord kept*
> *you with us until spring.*

There is a flicker in his eyes, his face moves into an expression beyond words. I feel his wife's eyes steady upon us. His son's silent disappearance from the kitchen frame speak the acknowledgement of the finality of the news.

All good things must come to an end...

All good things must come to an end...

We sit a long time then, tears welling up in me dropping onto my shirt and lap. His wife speaks. I am startled into the realization she knows something is not right but because of difficulty hearing she cannot fathom what is going on. I move swiftly to her side, kneeling beside her tiny frame perched on the edge of the sofa.

He is going to get better, isn't he?

I gather her hands in mine. She looks, searches my face, trembling. The small shake of my head is all she needs. She crumbles before me:

Oh no, oh no. I don't want. Oh no, Oh no.

She rocks and sobs and gazes at him who is her life and love for so many years, so many years.

Grace and peace to you
Grace and peace be unto you
from our Father and Lord Jesus Christ.

We are desperate O Lord,
in need of Your grace and Your peace.
Praise be the God and Father of our Lord Jesus
Christ,
The Father of mercies and God of all comfort,
Who comforts us in all our tribulation,
That we may comfort those who are in any trouble
With the comfort with which we ourselves are com-
forted by God. (adapted from 2 Corinthians 1:2-4,
HCSB)

Comfort in all tribulation. Comfort in any trouble.
You, Jesus are our Comfort, our only Comfort in
life.
...But we have this treasure in earthen vessels,
that the excellence of the power may be of God
and not of us.

We are hard pressed on every side, yet not crushed;
We are perplexed, but not in despair;
Persecuted, but not forsaken;
Struck down, but not destroyed—
Always carrying about in the body the dying
    of the Lord Jesus,
That the life of Jesus also may be manifested
    in our body.
For we who live are always delivered to death
    for Jesus' sake,
That the life of Jesus also may be manifested in our
mortal flesh. (adapted from 2 Corinthians 4:7-11,
NKJV)

Delivered to death for Jesus' sake, that the life of Jesus may be manifested in our mortal flesh? Eternity manifested in our mortal flesh?

> *How can that be, O God of gods?*
> *How can that be, O God of all comfort?*
> *How can that be, O God of mercies?*

It is by Your goodness expressed through Your kindness to us in Jesus Christ, in Jesus Christ. May the heavens proclaim Your glory. May all the earth praise Your name, for You are holy and You are good O Lord.

> **All good things must come to an end...**
> **Yet, Your love endures forever. You, O God en-**
> **dure forever.**

Silence

I have two questions.

She is solemn, supine in her bed, night cap framing her generous cocoa brown face sprinkled with dark freckles. Her eyes are filled up with concern and do not sparkle. Her mouth is set very still and almost trembles. We wait. It is a long, long silence.

I am surprised. The visit had been a routine one discussing a headache and not feeling well. The daughter was very concerned because she knew her mother was ill but nothing more. Her mother had quit talking to her. It was clear that the mother was upset with her. The cause of the upset was not apparent amongst the myriad of small things it could be. The silence was oppressive and unsettling. Both mother and daughter were bereft of comfort and joy.

This silence was a hard thing. Both women were left alone, out of society's mainstream: one because she was so elderly and bedbound and thought to have dementia, the other because she had had a massive stroke when young and was left with a significant hemiparesis. Their lives were one of routine: day to day sameness broken only by the loud rambunctious clamoring of a large, curly headed brown dog whose eyes you could not see. His abundant joy and carefree bounding blessed the daughter and irritated the mother. The bantering back and forth between the two of them was part of their lives. Its absence silenced the home into an oppressive dullness that not even the dog could break.

The headache of two weeks seemed almost constant, exacerbated by times when the daughter was gone. The spoken differences between the two were in choices of TV programs and the daughter's smoking and need to take a break from caregiving. All these things would mean she would not be with her mother.

What is it that you want? I asked.
Her not to be gone.
   She is not really gone.
Yes, she is.
   You mean even when she is in the kitchen that upsets you?
Yes.
   Oh, so you want her right here? Right here with you?

Yes…she nods her head toward a chair to the right of the foot of the bed where her daughter was sitting.

Right there? I ask.
Yes, right there.
Oh.

We talked then of the need for her daughter to have some time to herself. How silence was very upsetting. How Scripture spoke of being angry but not sinning in one's anger or allowing the sun to go down on one's anger. Her half nodding head made it clear she heard but that she was reticent to concede so easily. Her daughter's vigorously nodding head out of her mother's sight signified her affirmation. We adjusted medicines and were about to close with prayer when You prompted me, Lord to ask if she, the mother, had any questions. She looked at me, then looked away, far away. After a time, she said:

I have two questions.

We wait. It is a long, long silence. When the silence drags on and on, I wonder if she has lost her train of thought. You Lord, prompt her to speak.

I am not sure I want to ask you the questions.
Why?

The air in the room becomes still. Our breath seems to pause, waiting. She does not speak.

> *Are you afraid to ask me?*
> Her big eyes turn to me, then away. **Yes.**
> *Why?*

The question stays in the air. She shakes herself.

Next time, next time you come, I will ask.

I pull a chair to the bed, sit down, lean toward her and wait. The silence lingers.

> *Does it have to do with you?* I whisper.
> **Yes.**
> *Does it have to do with how long you might be here before you go home to the Lord?*
> She looks up startled. **Yes.**
> *What do you think?* I ask gently.
> **It won't be long now,** she whispers.
> *Are you afraid?*
> **Yes, in a way.**
> *Are you afraid to be alone, in case the Lord calls you home and no one is here with you?*
> **Yes,** she whispers.

Her daughter shifts in the chair. She understands immediately.

> *So when your daughter is not in that chair right there, it really upsets you?*

She nods.

> *Are you really alone when she is not here?*

She turns to me then, eyes meeting mine, questioning me without words.

> *You love the Lord?*

She nods vigorously.

He is with you always. You can always talk to Him.
She is not with Him. SHE is not with Him.

Her words burst forth shattering the stillness shattering her fearful silence. I am startled.

Who is not with Him?
Her, my mother.
Oh, where is she?
She is ceased. Her face begins to crumble.
Oh, did she love the Lord?
Oh yes, but she is not there anymore. She is not with Him anymore.

Her cries become a wailing. The deep moaning agony breaks into sobbing.

She does not talk to me anymore. She won't speak to me. She is not there anymore.

Her grieving unleashed slowly subsides into silence.

You loved your mother?
Yes. I loved her. I took care of her. I worshiped the ground on which she walked.

Her grief fills the room anew. You are so present, Lord, providing the stillness, the silence large enough to hold the grief. We sit, all of us, while You do Your work.

Mrs. Foster, what is the greatest commandment?
To love the Lord with all your heart, her voice trails off.
Yes, is God a jealous God?

She nods.

When you have a concern, who do you talk to?

My mother.
Oh, and does she talk to you?
Yes.
So that is why you have been so upset?
Yes.
And that makes your daughter being gone hard on
you?
Yes.
Mrs. Foster, tell me something, do you love your
mother more than you love the Lord?

She does not answer at first. The "yes" is murmured so low, I almost do not catch it.

Do you believe your mother loves you?
She nods in affirmation.
And you believe the Lord loves you?
She again nods yes.
If God asked you to do something, would you do it?
Yes.
I wonder if God has asked your mother to quit
speaking to you. She loves the Lord, she is His child,
nothing will ever separate her from God. It says so
in Scripture, in Romans and we can trust God who
promises.
She nods.
So if God told her not to talk to you, she would do
what He asked?
Yes, she nods.
Why do you think He would do that?

She needs me to repeat the question. Her face, bewildered is accompanied by a shrug.

Do you suppose God wants you to come to Him and
not to your mother? You are His daughter. You are

His beloved daughter. Do you suppose He wants to
have you come to Him and listen to Him?

She turns and looks at me, her face reflecting her hungry open heart.

He wants you, Mrs. Foster, He wants you. He loves
you that much.

She holds herself so still in that truth. Something deep begins to stir in her.

Let's talk with Him now, I gently offer.

So we pray, Lord … to You. You listen and You speak Your words of tender love. Your loving kindness compels us to repentance. As we pray and praise You Lord, she begins to move her hand. She is touched by Your Holy Spirit and she lifts her hand in worship.

Praise You Lord Jesus. Praise You, she cries out.
You are so good. You are so good.

She shakes her head and lifts her hands and cries out.

So many doors are open now, you opened so
many doors, she cries.
The Lord opened the doors dear. The Lord did.
I can go with You now, she calls out to You.
I can go with You.

We stay in worshipful adoration of You, Lord. She looks around the room, her eyes rest on her daughter whose humble presence has been with her mother this whole time. I gently ask her:

The silence from your mother so upset you, what do
you think your silence to your daughter is doing?
Upsetting her, she whispers.
Yes, and life is too short (she nods) *to spend your*
days doing that.

After a moment of quiet I rise; she glances over to me.

Thank you.

No, thank God. He has done a magnificent thing.

She nods and looks away. A flood of Your presence fills her anew and she is shaken with tears of gratitude and praise to You. We share hugs, silent ones in You, long ones, side by side, cheek to cheek, in Your glory. You are so good, Lord. You are so good.

Yea, though I walk through the valley
    of the shadow of death,
I shall fear no evil. For You are with me.
    You are with me.
(adapted from Psalms 23:4, KJV)

He Calls Them Each by Name

The house sits alongside all the other houses on this very busy street but it is not like all the other houses. It is different. It is different in the overhanging awning that shelters the large front porch whose furniture speaks of days and evenings in the warmth of spring and summer where sharing and laughter filled many hearts. It is different in the caring love in which stepping stones were placed at precise intervals to guide one from driveway to porch: the well-tended stones welcoming one into the shelter of the big porch. It is different in the two doorbells at the front door which give one pause to ponder which to push, how long and how often.

The earnest woman who answered the door had eyes, big and solemn that twinkled with life, her short hair graced a face that was both bold and beautiful, refined in an elegant way that spoke to the character of the mother who had taught her to be. That first visit was for late morning; I was even later than morning, closer to lunch. The lady of the house had just risen and it was not appropriate for me to see her before she had tended to her morning ritual of bathroom, bathing, dressing and having settled herself in mind and spirit to welcome someone into her space. This was after all her domain. Her daughter explained the need for a delay; but I offered that it was okay for I saw people in any state of preparedness. She was hesitant. Later I was to understand her hesitation more fully as one of honoring her mother and desiring simultaneously to accommodate the professional's need to conserve time.

I climbed the stairs, turning at the mid-landing to ascend the remaining stairs to the large upstairs foyer. She was standing with her walker; gown askew, hair standing at attention. On seeing me, she stopped, drew herself up very tall and shot me this look. I stopped and recognized instantly my mistake. She was queen and I was there on her permission. She would perform her ablutions and I would wait as an act of honor and respect. We, her daughter and I, retired then downstairs, drinking water that was different, special, cold, refreshing with a distinct crispness that underlined the elegance of this home, these people, and their way of living. I sighed silently in appreciation of both water and Your way Lord of making me aware of Your timing and way of being.

The front upstairs room was like a small kingdom; everything that was needed to live was there. She who dwelled there had been quite content to settle, allowing others to replenish her with fresh food, clean clothes and company. She rarely left, others were drawn to her to honor her, whom they loved and admired so much. The TV was on, a tennis match was being played; it was muted to allow for concentration.

She turned a freshly washed face to me; her hair was brushed back revealing a face that was alight with laughter, pride, and stubbornness.

How are you? she huskily inquired.
I am fine.

I wanted to laugh; she had stolen my line. I had been gently placed where I needed to be in her presence, cognizant at all times of her dignity, her beauty both within and without. Her character revealed that she saw, heard and experienced life in such a way that it deepened the very essence of woman, the best of woman in her.

Her words though measured and precise carried a hint of laughter. At any moment, a personally created word would erupt; we would all succumb to laughter that wells up from deep within our beings, laughter, welling up out of the recognition of the sage insightfulness and delightful wit of this queen who was due utmost respect. The banter between her and her youngest daughter was a mixture of tugging and pulling, truth-telling and expressed surprise in her face and eyes as answers were explored to the many questions I had to find out her physical, emotional and spiritual condition.

She had no interest in food. She had no interest in going downstairs. She had no interest in going out. Why? I asked.

I don't need to.

The silence that followed spoke to my loss at how to respond. She must have laughed silently then; another tiny victory not necessarily over me, but over life itself. We spoke of possibilities then as we would many times at subsequent visits. She remained observant of me, watchful. I felt I was being held at the outskirts of her kingdom, being allowed momentary glimpses into the treasures of her life. Then I asked, as is my custom, if I could pray with her, say a blessing for her.

Her sharp glance spoke of her surprise that was simultaneously contained and dignified. She offered her hand and we prayed to You, Lord, who are the Creator of all of life, to You who know time and the moment of that day before the beginning of time. We prayed to You, who know this woman, every hair on her head just as much as You know every star…its name and place. We prayed for Your grace, Your love to fill her that she might live the days of her life fully in You, knowing You, reveling in Your love, fulfilling Your purpose, glorifying You in all that she did. We prayed for Your wisdom to enable me to make the right medical decision for her best well-being. We gave You thanks for life and breath and all those we love. We gave thanks for You Lord most of all.

At the Amen, I looked up; her eyes steady upon me did not waver. She contemplated me awhile. I felt her draw me into her presence, into her heart, into her precious space; she welcomed me as one of her own.

We had so many visits after that. The joy of visiting that home and sharing life with her, her husband, her son, and particularly her three wonderful daughters were always ones filled with laughter, celebration, and deep presence to each other: a rubbing of souls together that creates a bond that cannot be seen or touched but only felt deep in the heart. We had many light moments and many, many times the "look" that stopped one cold was shot from her, the elegant queen. Whatever it was we were doing had to be stopped and adjusted to be more fitting to her whose dignity we honored. There was rarely a complaint and those that were expressed were ones during the times where the body's most basic cares and needs were being examined and cared for: tender skin, private places, bodily functions that were not paying attention to the elegance of the woman who desired them to stay properly in place. Yet her dignity always remained in the midst of the laughter and good-natured response to the prodding of daughters about her needing to be checked and her heretofore, guarded privacy being interrupted so that she could be cared for properly according to her standard for all of life. Even in the midst of great pain, emotional or physical, she remained quietly present: dignified, caring, elegant before us and before You, O Lord.

The last visit was hard. The unexpectedly rapid downhill course took me by surprise. I had grown accustomed to the warm afternoon visits, the bantering, the shared camaraderie of laughing at life, at death, at ourselves all the while maintaining this dignity of being that can only truly come in groundedness in You. She was silent in spirit and voice when she turned her face to me. It was apparent that pain had taken its toll. The disinterest in food had reached that final level and the lack of sustenance shone in the sunkenness of her eyes and cheeks.

Oh I felt myself say within, placing my bag down indifferently at my feet. Nothing medical was really needed, not now. I struggled, willing my tears not to well up, not to perch at the edges of my eyelids, not to fall, one by one on the bed clothes as I held her hand and slid into sitting with her. She closed her eyes. We sat in silence a long time, her hand in mine; her kingdom and presence gently laid aside to allow You, the author of every heartbeat and breath to step in proclaiming Your glory and Your love more loudly than ever before. Her small hand lay in mine. Her pulse thready, waxing and waning, her eyes occasionally would open, gaze at me then close again. The tears would not stay where they were supposed to. I sensed her seeing me and giving me permission to grieve.

We prayed: her and her daughters and I to You. We prayed bound together, sisters in You. Your presence bathed us, held us, comforted us. As I sat in the silence that followed, there was a sense of someone compelling me to look up. My hand was pulled toward her face; I bent closer to look intently into her deep, dark eyes. They shone with penetration that reflects the deep of oneself calling out to the deep of another: our eyes locked and very clearly, with great dignity, she said:

Thank you.

Ah Lord, my God, how great is Your Holy Name. You Who have marshaled the heavens into place and have flung out every star, placing them where they are to be, calling them each by name, You have shone Your glory. We have seen it. We acknowledge Your calling upon this beloved daughter of Yours to Your home which You had prepared for her all this time. We walk with her into Your presence and bow down at Your feet. All the saints are around You, clapping and clapping...and we hear Your joy, Your laughter: we hear Your joy, Your laughter in seeing Your daughter home.

> "To whom will you compare me? Or who is My
> equal?" says the Holy One.
> Lift your eyes and looked to the heavens:
>   Who created all these?
> He who brings out the starry host one by one,
>   and calls them each by name,
> Because of His great power and mighty strength,
> not one of them is missing...
>
> Do you not know? Have you not heard?
> The LORD is the everlasting God,
>   the Creator of the ends of the earth.
> He will not grow tired or weary,
>   and His understanding no one can fathom.

He gives strength to the weary and increases the
power of the weak.

Even youths grow tired and weary,
    and young men stumble and fall;
But those who wait on the LORD
    will renew their strength.
They will soar on wings like eagles;
    they will run and not grow weary,
They will walk and not be faint.
(adapted from Isaiah 40:25-26; 28-31, NIV, NKJV)

You Are My Friend

It has been a long journey breathing through good and bad times with lungs that have struggled because they cannot expand or stretch, cannot really fill with air and life. It speaks of the destructive power of cigarettes, of smoke and of choice.

The confinement began years ago, so long ago that the light of the sun and the breath of fresh air have become distant scents brought in by an occasional visitor mixed at times with the smells of perfume or lotion. The confinement has been hard...both for him and his wife. At the first visit three years ago, it was the names that created a dilemma. He desired to be called by his shortened first name and he would call me by my professional title and last name. It often, however, was changed to Dr. Jude.

Perhaps it was the recognition of the strength of the character of the man both in spirit and heart, in spite of the confinement to a bed-to-chair existence. Perhaps, it was the need for a strict professional attitude during many heated, drawn out discussions about how he wanted to be treated and my belief that his plan was medically unsound. His medical expert opinion was grounded in the fact that he knew his body far better than anyone including me and far better than the knowledge of countless faceless individuals whose statistics and research concerning treatment and expected response did not matter at all when it came to knowing oneself. Whatever it was, I always called him Mr. Sherman.

He amazingly graduated from hospice four times: always managing to take a downhill course then stuttering to a plateau and staying the same for months...years. It was a noticeable change one visit: the sharp attention to detail and arguments against any recommendations was met with some difficulty in remembering. Hesitation accompanied by long pauses when he tried to recollect what he was saying and what point he was making became painfully more frequent. Then, just as suddenly, as if by Your divine intervention, he would pick up right where he had gotten stuck as if nothing had happened.

Lord, You had given him a gift for detail. He took it to an extreme: knowing it, pursuing it, wanting it, exacting it from others at cost. His whole life had been filled with the detail of his work, his illness, his body, historic events and scientific trivia with seemingly one aim: to control outcome. By Your grace Lord, he was conceding little by little, day by day that his control was not necessary or necessarily a good thing. The shrug of his shoulders in not remembering to take all his medicine and cheerful: "Oh well, that's life!" with a peal of laughter, revealed evidence of the mighty working of Your grace in his life.

The loss of mental acuity was incremental; the bounding back to almost full capacity time and again, amazingly reflecting his resilience, his resilience in life, in living. Even when it seemed he was most unable, he would reminisce and share a story ripe with detail. It never failed to cause him to smile and hesitate at the punch lines and laugh...laugh a good long laugh before finishing.

In all visits, he, so thin, would sit upright with a navy blue-covered wedge cushion behind his back, pulling occasionally on the overhang bar to set himself straight. His shirts thinned to the point of translucency: his left shirt pocket always filled with a pad of paper, a writing utensil or two ready, ready to be used. He never used the things in his shirt pocket during any of the visits I had with him, but he was always ready... always ready...even as death approached.

Are you scared? I query.
No, not really.

He is quiet, breathing heavily between sentences. He ponders the question and his response. His words, measured, are often interrupted for long periods of pursed lip breathing.

I have asked the Lord for two things, he says.

We wait; his wife, standing at the door pensively listening and I, sitting on his bed leaning forward. With his increasing difficulty in hearing and labored voice, we strain at times to hear and to make our responses heard.

One thing... (long pause)**...is that I wanted to get to six score and three.**

A dramatic eyebrow raise and glimmer of a smile hold us in suspense:

I am seventy two. And the other...

The wait oh so long, is filled with patient silence.

The other...that by God's grace, I would be.

His face is serious, thoughtful. His words rest in and around us, echoing the Apostle Paul in 1 Corinthians 5:10:

**But by the grace of God
I am what I am and
His grace which was bestowed upon me was
not in vain.**

It is not a mistake. He has finished the sentence...as I ponder his words, he regards me solemnly. He starts with a favorite familiar line of his:

**Do you remember? Do you remember when
you first came here so long ago?
Do you remember when I asked you some
things? Do you remember what I asked you?**

My mind races, there is no way to remember either the day or the words. He enjoys my confusion and hesitancy, letting the embarrassment of my not remembering make its mark.

Tell me, I say, very seriously.

**I told you that I wanted you to call me by my
first name like all my friends.**

The silence is dramatic. I am taken off guard. There are no
words to say to this man gentled by Your grace, weakened by illness,
preparing to come home to You. I look steadfastly into his eyes,
helpless, unable to speak. He leans forward and whispers gently:

Do you not want to be my friend?

His gaze never wavers; his hand near mine closes over with a
gentle touch. My tears well up and begin to fall one after the other
onto his bed sheets. I am unable to speak. With effort, I whisper:

Yes, Mr. Sherman, I am your friend...

And we both laugh through tears at the so familiar habit of
address.

I think we should pray.

In Your presence, in Your grace I hear Your words to Your
beloved disciples:

I have called you friends. (John 15:15)

A great sorrow and a great thanksgiving for Your grace and
the power of Your gentling love rises to overflowing. The tears fall
afresh and the hand of the one who is friend catches them with
open palm. We pray in thanksgiving to You, for Your faithfulness,
for Your grace, for the power of being friend in You, Jesus. You,
Lord say:

This is My commandment, that you love one another,
As I have loved you. Greater love has no man than this,
That a man lay down his life for his friends.
You are My friends, if you do whatsoever
    I command you.
Henceforth, I call you not servants;
For the servant does not know what his Lord does:
But I have called you friends;

For all things that I have heard of My Father,
I have made known to you.
You have not chosen Me, but I have chosen you.
(adapted from John 15:12-16a, KJV)

Also from Energion Publications

Within these pages you will fi nd practical and compassionate words, along with hands and a heart that knows the pain of loss and feet that are willing to accompany the reader on their journey.

The Beatitudes from Christ's Sermon on the Mount are more than beautiful, even puzzling words. They can be your anchor when the waves roll and the winds howl.

More from Energion Publications

Personal Study
Holy Smoke! Unholy Fire	Bob McKibben	$14.99
The Jesus Paradigm	David Alan Black	$17.99
When People Speak for God	Henry Neufeld	$17.99
The Sacred Journey	Chris Surber	$11.99

Christian Living
It's All Greek to Me	David Alan Black	$3.99
Grief: Finding the Candle of Light	Jody Neufeld	$8.99
My Life Story	Becky Lynn Black	$14.99
Crossing the Street	Robert LaRochelle	$16.99
Life as Pilgrimage	David Moffett-Moore	14.99

Bible Study
Learning and Living Scripture	Lentz/Neufeld	$12.99
From Inspiration to Understanding	Edward W. H. Vick	$24.99
Philippians: A Participatory Study Guide	Bruce Epperly	$9.99
Ephesians: A Participatory Study Guide	Robert D. Cornwall	$9.99
Ecclesiastes: A Participatory Study Guide	Russell Meek	$9.99

Theology
Creation in Scripture	Herold Weiss	$12.99
Creation: the Christian Doctrine	Edward W. H. Vick	$12.99
The Politics of Witness	Allan R. Bevere	$9.99
Ultimate Allegiance	Robert D. Cornwall	$9.99
History and Christian Faith	Edward W. H. Vick	$9.99
The Journey to the Undiscovered Country	William Powell Tuck	$9.99
Process Theology	Bruce G. Epperly	$4.99

Ministry
Clergy Table Talk	Kent Ira Groff	$9.99
Out of This World	Darren McClellan	$24.99

Generous Quantity Discounts Available
Dealer Inquiries Welcome
Energion Publications — P.O. Box 841
Gonzalez, FL 32560
Website: http://energionpubs.com
Phone: (850) 525-3916

CPSIA information can be obtained
at www.ICGtesting.com
Printed in the USA
FFOW05n0955190816

9 781631 992469